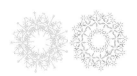

A SELECTION FROM
THE WAY FORWARD
HOLIDAY READING LIST

WITH BEST WISHES

Prentiss C. Burt

J.P.Morgan

THE LAST
AMATEURS

Mark de Rond

THE LAST AMATEURS

TO HELL AND BACK WITH THE CAMBRIDGE BOAT RACE CREW

ICON BOOKS

Published in the UK in 2008 by
Icon Books Ltd, The Old Dairy, Brook Road,
Thriplow, Cambridge SG8 7RG
email: info@iconbooks.co.uk
www.iconbooks.co.uk

Sold in the UK, Europe, South Africa and Asia
by Faber & Faber Ltd, 3 Queen Square,
London WC1N 3AU or their agents

Distributed in the UK, Europe, South Africa and Asia
by TBS Ltd, TBS Distribution Centre, Colchester Road
Frating Green, Colchester CO7 7DW

This edition published in Australia in 2008
by Allen & Unwin Pty Ltd,
PO Box 8500, 83 Alexander Street,
Crows Nest, NSW 2065

Distributed in Canada by Penguin Books Canada,
90 Eglinton Avenue East, Suite 700,
Toronto, Ontario M4P 2YE

ISBN: 978-184831-015-5

Typeset in 11½ on 15 pt Sabon by Wayzgoose

Printed in the UK by
CPI Mackays, Chatham, ME5 8TD

CONTENTS

About the Author

Mark de Rond is an Oxford-educated Cambridge fellow. His work on Cambridge's preparations for the Boat Race has featured in *Time*, the *Economist*, *The Times*, *The Week*, the *Financial Times*, the *Guardian*, and on BBC Radio 4, the BBC World Service and TalkSPORT.

for Shelby and Dylan

Be daring, be different, be impractical, be anything that will assert integrity of purpose and imaginative vision against the play-it-safers, the creatures of the commonplace, the slaves of the ordinary.

Cecil Beaton

If you can keep your head when all about you
Are losing theirs and blaming it on you;
If you can trust yourself when all men doubt you,
But make allowance for their doubting too;
If you can wait and not be tired by waiting,
Or, being lied about, don't deal in lies,
Or, being hated, don't give way to hating,
And yet don't look too good, nor talk too wise;

If you can dream – and not make dreams your master;
If you can think – and not make thoughts your aim;
If you can meet with triumph and disaster
And treat those two imposters just the same;
If you can bear to hear the truth you've spoken
Twisted by knaves to make a trap for fools,
Or watch the things you gave your life to broken,
And stoop and build 'em up with worn-out tools;

If you can make one heap of all your winnings
And risk it on one turn of pitch-and-toss,
And lose, and start again at your beginnings
And never breathe a word about your loss;
If you can force your heart and nerve and sinew
To serve your turn long after they are gone,
And so hold on when there is nothing in you
Except the Will which says to them: 'Hold on';

If you can talk with crowds and keep your virtue,
Or walk with kings – nor lose the common touch;
If neither foes nor loving friends can hurt you;
If all men count with you, but none too much;
If you can fill the unforgiving minute
With sixty seconds' worth of distance run –
Yours is the Earth and everything that's in it,
And – which is more – you'll be a Man, my son!

Rudyard Kipling

ACKNOWLEDGEMENTS

This book would not exist without the support of Duncan Holland and the 2006–07 Cambridge University Boat Race squad. Duncan not only provided me with unrestricted access to the squad and coaching team; he also opened a window to the ups and downs of coaching life, his feats but also flaws, the coups but more often than not terrible challenges of trying to coach a group of world-class athletes, and allowed me to write openly about them.

This same appreciation applies to Tom James, Rebecca, Thorsten, Seb, Kieran, Pete, Jake, Dan, Kip, Russ, David Billings, Colin, Wanne, Ali, Tobias, Don, Oli, Doug, Pat, Marco, Richard, Dave Hopper and David Barst. Tom James, in particular, in his role as President of the CUBC, has been enormously supportive of my presence within the club, and it's not easy to express the extent of my appreciation. He is the classic example of a British oarsman of international stature, a leader of men without being unnecessarily forceful or authoritative, and a friend. His successor, Dan O'Shaughnessy, was equally supportive of this project and generous in allowing me to write candidly about his experiences too.

I have also really appreciated the friendships extended to me by the assistant coaches Rob Baker, Grant Craies, Donald Legget and Tim McLaren, as well as such Old Blues as Chris Dalley, David Gillard, Martin Haycock, Wayne Pommen, David Searle and Quintus Travis, the club's physiotherapist Linda Dennis, its secretary Richard Pryce-Jones and its senior member Paul Luzio. My 'townie' rowing friends too have been supportive, particularly Martin Childs, Mary Phenna, Barney Price and James Curran. My appreciation goes out to them for allowing me to write about our Boston adventures. Likewise my thanks go to the Darwin College fellowship and my departmental colleagues who patiently endured my long and unexplained absences, especially Tim Bellis, Jochen Runde, Arnoud De Meyer and Willy Brown. I thank Xchanging, our corporate sponsor, without whom there might not have been a 2007 Boat Race, the Fulbright Commission, Stanford University,

James March, Robert Burgelman, Paul Sargent, Margo Beth Crouppen, the Espin family for their generosity and hospitality, Peter Drury of ITV, Sophie Pickford, Phil Searle and Howard Guest for allowing me to use their photographs, United Agents for allowing me to quote from *The Office*, by Ricky Gervais and Stephen Merchant, and Twentieth Century Fox for allowing me to quote from an episode of *24* written by Howard Gordon and David Fury. Thanks too go to Peter, Andrew, Simon, Duncan and Sarah at Icon Books for taking this project on board. This is an independent book that required a like-minded publisher.

I'm not sure this book would be as readable without the input of my wife Roxana. She patiently read through several versions (the earliest of which were abysmally poor), pencil in hand, and the manuscript is the better, and the more honest, for it.

I hope this book will give you some enjoyment. The occasional bit might take you by surprise. After all, it's the story of a club without equal – one that is enduring yet fragile, sacred yet not without profanity, perfect and yet so very human too—

By way of introduction

This manuscript is designed to be evocative rather than scholarly. That said, the ethnographic research on which it draws is every bit as rigorous as might be expected from an academic tome (but without the usual pomp and circumstance). Though ethnography will never be free of impartiality, the occasional reference to the author allows one to see observer and subject co-evolve – often tentatively and clumsily.

Nowhere is this relation between subject and observer more poignantly expressed than in David Lodge's novel *Small World*, using the metaphor of a striptease:

> The dancer teases the audience, as the text teases its readers, with the promise of an ultimate revelation that is infinitely postponed. Veil after veil, garment after garment, is removed, but it is the delay in the stripping that makes it exciting, not the stripping itself; because no sooner has one secret been revealed than we lose interest in it and crave another. When we have seen the girl's underwear we want to see her body, when we have seen her breasts we want to see her buttocks, and when we have seen her buttocks we want to see her pubis, and when we see her pubis, the dance ends – but is our curiosity and desire satisfied? Of course not. The vagina remains hidden within the girl's body, shaded by her pubic hair, and even if she were to spread her legs before us it would still not satisfy the curiosity and desire set into motion by the stripping. Staring into the orifice we find that

we have somehow overshot the goal of our quest, gone beyond pleasure in contemplating beauty; gazing into the womb we are returned to the mystery of our own origins.[1]

As it happens, I did actually try to write myself out of the story, and might have got away with it too. The result would have been the one masquerading for the many, a particular voice mistaken for the megaphone of a society. It would have been dishonest. For it is thus that the reader becomes privy to the writer's experience, receiving (in the words of *Harper's* editor) 'direct confirmation of its truth value'.

There is thus a strong subtext to the narrative. There are several, in fact. Depending on the reader's background and interests, it can be read as a realist sports book (in supplying a warts-and-all account of the 2007 Cambridge Boat Race crew), as a business book (as it articulates important traits of high-performance teams), as an ethnography (specifically designed to tease at the boundary of ethnography and auto-ethnography, as well as a gender ethnography), or as an example of C. Wright Mills' 'sociological imagination' (in highlighting the temporal and dialectical nature of high-performance teams).

Or you can just enjoy it for what it is, the story of a young academic hopelessly lost in his own project: an attempt to do justice to the visceral nature of Boat Race preparation, preserving all that's genteel about Cambridge yet cracking the seal to reveal what lies beneath – a world both ordinary and exotic – redeeming its splendid yet flawed, hypercompetitive student oarsmen and, in the process, atoning for himself.

FOREWORD

I love tradition. History and passion make sport what it is. The Boat Race has this and more. It is seen worldwide to be the most significant challenge of all Varsity sport at the two universities. The professionalism of the chief coach and his team of coaches, the support staff and numerous advisors in almost every area of sporting excellence help to ensure that everything possible has been done to aid the crew's preparation in what is a race of amateurs. No stone is left unturned.

This book gives you a unique insight into the training, preparation, stresses and strains on all who are involved. What you have to realise is that every individual has their own motivation: a story about why they are trying to make the final crew, committing themselves to train at least twice a day for six months. Alongside their training, each rower must complete their studies (there is no allowance for being a Blue); this adds extra challenges and brings extra pressure to each individual.

International rowing is about trying to get the best possible result. So is the Boat Race, but there is a difference. At the Olympic Games it is possible to win gold, silver and bronze; for some people these honours may be out of reach. Making the final or even getting to the Games itself is an incredible achievement. The Boat Race is completely different. The glory is in winning; there are no silver medals, there is no second place – you win or you lose. Defeat is taken extremely hard, not just as an individual or as the whole crew. The disappointment is felt by everyone involved, and even past Blues. In some strange way that is what makes the Boat Race so special.

During the build-up to the race in early spring there is a sense of pride in Blue Boat athletes, an ambition to do your college and university proud. There is a respectful hate for the opposition. It's not until the race is over and you become an Old Blue that the realisation of what you have been part of sinks in. A small piece of history has been written and you were part of it.

I always find it a little bizarre during the week of the Boat Race when Old Blues change character, turning back into young men, reliving their moment from Boat Races gone by – often people who have achieved in whatever field they followed after university.

This race gets a huge amount of media coverage. For most of the people involved it will be their biggest day in the media spotlight, but the nice thing about it is that if there were no media interest, no spotlight, the race between these two universities would still go on and mean as much to the individuals who actually race.

Sir Steve Redgrave CBE

CHAPTER 1

I'm about to let you in on a secret. Beneath these pages lies a world in black and white.[2] It's one rarely seen by the public, yet one that for two centuries has been a preparatory ground for industrialists and politicians, the makers and sometimes shakers of our fragile society. It's here that Evelyn Waugh's pretty *Brideshead Revisited* meets the frazzled *Fight Club* world of Chuck Palahniuk: a flamboyant world with heroes and villains all of its own and dominated by a single event: the Boat Race.

For this is the true story of thirty-odd Cambridge students risking all for a rare chance to race their Oxford rivals over four muddy miles of water and to be forever called a *Blue*. Their tale reinforces the splendour and chivalry that are the Cambridge University Boat Club, but also serves to give it that elusive human face. For despite their brilliance, these individuals are flawed too – stoic but self-centred, affectionate but exploitative: that which makes them good making them difficult too. Reality, after all, wouldn't be what it is, would it, without rough edges and sharp corners.

So what does it take to earn one's place in this Varsity race? Why would these students swap dreaming spires for still dark mornings, for perpetual exhaustion, for rain and wind and damp clothes? Why would anyone pursue anything where the personal investment is so very steep and yet the material reward non-existent? To train to remain forever an amateur?

The answers are far from straightforward – or so I discovered when joining the squad as an ethnographer on their first day of training. The experience of living with them was to become a period of sharp contrasts – one in which that critical and usually distinct boundary between what is real and what is imagined ceases to exist; where nightmares and wacky visions rob one of any sense of place and time; where I was to question (quite unexpectedly) the idea of what it is to be a man among men, physiologically inferior and, despite an Oxbridge education, intellectually matched if not outright bested here too; to look, with Coleridge, at my soul with a telescope.[3]

And so there are really two stories to be told. There is the one about the oarsmen and then there is the one about me in relation to them. Of these, mine is the more difficult to pin down, if only because I no longer see the forest for the trees. But write it down I must if there is to be any hope of showing what is going on inside the lives and minds of these amateurs. For how else am I to magnify the splendour and vulgarity of them that sacrifice all at the altar of self? To trap their demons and nail down the possibility of meaningfulness?

The story begins on a September day like any other, eighteen hours before the 2007 Boat Race campaign is to start. After three agonising months of uncertainty, I finally get word that permission is granted for me to go native with the squad and to participate in their everyday lives as they train and prepare to select a crew to race Oxford. I was to examine their lives from the inside, so to speak, but to do so in the detached fashion of a 'scientist'. For that is what ethnographers do: we study people by living with them, by participating in their everyday lives so as to try to understand why they do what they do and why this makes sense to them.* Like the ethnographer Kate Fox (*Watching the English*), writing about them, to me, often felt like that children's game where you try to

---

*The earliest ethnographers were concerned with non-Western societies. These were often thought of as primitive or exotic. It's only comparatively recently that ethnographers have applied their tools to understanding their own, often Western, social environs.

pat your head and rub your tummy at the same time: trying simultaneously to be like them and yet fiercely to defend whatever scrap of no-man's-land remains between them and you – between the real world and the world of science. It's little wonder then that we occasionally stand accused of having become too intimately involved with our subjects – guilty of losing that neutrality and objectivity that are the hallmarks of science proper, and rendering our work of little or no scholarly value.

> Shakespeare drew a map of the human mind as clearly as Newton mapped the heavens. Why is one considered science and the other fit only to be mocked with jokes about pretty girls and Drury Lane?[4]

Social life cannot be replicated in a test-tube, and thus the difficulty remains of verifying that people actually say what it is they saw, and thought, and experienced. Is this a blessing or curse for the discipline of ethnography? A nice (and rather famous) example is entailed in an address by the late anthropologist Clifford Geertz to the American Academy. In it, he reflects on what 'going native' really means, and how reliable ethnographic descriptions might be. He used Bronislaw Malinowski's controversial *A Diary in the Strict Sense of the Term* as his point source – a meticulous record of time spent by Malinowski observing natives. This diary revealed a quite different world from that described in his authoritative text on the Western Pacific. And it was this diary, said Geertz, that blew the straw house of ethnography to bits, leaving its author accused of doing the dirty on the discipline. As Geertz pointed out, most of the shock arose from the discovery that Malinowski was not, to put it delicately, an unmitigated nice guy. He had rude things to say about the natives he was living with and rude words to say them in. He spent a great deal of his time wishing he were elsewhere.

Presumably Malinowski didn't care – he was dead by the time his wife published his diary. The controversy they triggered, however (he by writing and she by publishing it), points to a persistent difficulty in the practice of ethnography: to what extent are those doing the observing really able to engage with those being observed? Can they really ever perceive, feel, and think like a native? Are not all tainted by prejudice, likes and dislikes; by fears, insecurities, and loyalties; by indigestion and bad moods, euphoria and pleasure and wanting to be found pleasurable?

And yet ethnography seems to have so much going for it too. What better way to understand a community than to immerse oneself in it and by participation and observation and old-fashioned long-hand notes gradually sketch a portrait of it? To pursue a science in which the body and its senses actively partici-pate in the production of knowledge – an approach that takes seri-ously the fact that researcher and subject alike are before anything else beings of flesh and frayed nerves and emotions? To be able to pick up scents of tripe and damp in George Orwell's mining com-munities (*The Road to Wigan Pier*); of smoke and stout in Kate Fox's English pubs (*Pubwatching with Desmond Morris*); of sweat and leather in Loïc Wacquant's boxing gym (*Body and Soul*); of weed in Tom Wolfe's psychedelic 1960s (*The Electric Kool-Aid Acid Test*); of fear and loathing in William Whyte's Italian-American slum of Boston (*Street Corner Society*) or in Alexander Masters' poignant description of one homeless life (*Stuart: A Life Backwards*). Are there things more vivid or more colourful or even more sorrowful in this pen-and-paper universe?

Intoxicated by such heady fare, I take the plunge – lock, stock and barrel – into the jealously guarded world of Cambridge rowing. Little do I realise that my experience as ethnographer will prove among the least useful, and that my survival within the squad will come to hinge critically on my skills in conflict resolution. This was to become one of two surprising discoveries – the other being the realisation that by watching these young men in training I'd be facing my own reflection, seeing in them everything that I am not: virility, masculinity, youth, beauty, foolishness. I wasn't given a choice in the matter. For the self is never really left behind. Joining these students wasn't to be a turning away from the existential dilemmas of life – it was, as Geertz anticipated, to plunge into the midst of them. For to write non-fiction creatively, even about 'the other', is to descend into oneself, is to join Joseph Conrad in identifying 'our own sense of delight and wonder, pity and pain, and finding that latent feeling of fellowship with all creation'.

So what you have here is an account of the becoming of a Boat Race crew, one that wants very much to include all and everything but invariably reflects the flaws and daubs of the one doing the watching. Then again, understanding the inner lives of these rowers is not like reading a set of instructions, a repair manual or a cookbook. It's like Geertz said: more like grasping a proverb, catching an illusion, seeing a joke or reading a poem.

Just so.

CHAPTER 2

Speed is a function of rhythm. And rhythm in a crew is surprisingly tangible. It's that easy, predictable, relentless, nothing-else-matters-no-matter-what feel of the boat – a separation of stroke and recovery, a flawless coordination of lungs and legs, of push and let go, of brace and release: a wedlock of oarsman and boat, of oarsman and coxswain, each stroke an investment with the certainty of a return.

This rhythm is designed to generate flow, that most enviable of experiences – one familiar to many yet extraordinarily difficult to call up at will. It captures that rare moment in time where one is totally absorbed in what one is doing. It's the experience of pure harmony, or that point at which mind and matter fuse effortlessly and you know that something special has just occurred.[5]

Flow is said to lift experience from the ordinary to the optimal, to a Zen-like state, and it's in precisely those moments that we feel truly alive and in tune with what we are doing. For the oarsman, it's an experience in which the self merges with the act of rowing and becomes indistinguishable from it. Where anxiety, self-doubt, indeed self-consciousness itself has been cut out as if by a clever surgeon – a feeling that John Steinbeck described as very near to a kind of unconsciousness – where time changes its manner and where minutes disappear into the cloud of time. A time where everything finally falls into place: a groovy sensation of weightlessness yet total control, being really and truly alive in the present and knowing that nothing else matters, at least not now. Even as crowds roar, cameras flash, helicopters swivel dizzily overhead ...

yet none of it matters much. All that matters, the only thing that matters, is being right here right now – a rare glimpse of perfection.

The rhythm of a boat is like the beating of a heart: a platform upon which everything depends and all else becomes aligned. It is the condition on which flow depends – on which it feeds. And in a very real sense, it is the unremitting quest for rhythm and flow that helps explain the controversial choice to replace a brash but experienced American coxswain with one much less experienced, British and female. It explains why the five most experienced rowers questioned matters of selection, insisting that a Canadian oarsman be selected despite him being less competent than the Brit he would unseat.

It explains why Cambridge won the Boat Race, and why it nearly lost.

CHAPTER 3

Some things are surprisingly straightforward. Take the Boat Race result: you win or you lose. There's no such thing as runner-up, and even the margins are immaterial. Instead, the result is at once objective and public. What formally remains a private affair between the universities of Oxford and Cambridge has become one for mass consumption. Over a quarter of a million spectators line the muddy riverbanks in late March or early April each year to catch a glimpse of the spectacle. Those wishing to see all 4¼ miles of it rely on ITV's watchful eye, joining forces with a guestimated 120 million aficionados via cable or satellite. Goodness knows how many more tune in to the radio broadcast worldwide. The race 'was born with the silver spoon of popularity in its mouth',[6] and its soft spot with the public, not just in Britain but far afield, presents a problem to which no one has ever been able to give a satisfactory solution.[7]

Why does this race continue to hold such universal appeal? Is it because it involves two of the world's oldest and grandest institutions, the intellectual homes of Nobel laureates, philosophers, mathematicians and politicians? Of cerebral wizards like Isaac Newton, Lewis Carroll, John Maynard Keynes, W. H. Auden, C. S. Lewis, Isaiah Berlin and (once-upon-a-time coxswain) Stephen Hawking? Is it the secrecy surrounding crew selection and race preparation? Or is it because it has always been a thing of sharp contrasts: at once passionately amateur and yet holding to professional standards, exhibiting mutual respect yet intense rivalry too, where it's all about taking part but where the pain of losing is intolerable? Something that is terribly elite and yet of keen interest to every stratum of society? Quintessentially British though clones of it exist everywhere? Is it the all-or-nothing character of the race, as described by Oxford Blue (and four-time Olympic gold medallist) Matthew Pinsent?

> You must have huge courage to put yourself through all that is required to earn your seat, and row the race. There's something very alluring about putting yourself through all that, in order to row a race where the prize is a small medal in a little box. The pain is so worthwhile, but the penalties for losing are really high too. In other walks of life there is much to achieve even if you don't win, whereas in the Boat Race it's all or nothing.[8]

The race is rowed with the incoming tide from Putney to Mortlake in slim racing boats (also called shells), mostly made nowadays of carbon-fibre reinforced plastic. Each boat is manned by nine athletes *in statu pupillari* (full-time students). Eight of these are caught up in one of the most painful endurance sports imaginable for 4 miles and 374 yards on a whimsical, coffee-coloured course. After all, rowing requires not just cardiovascular fitness but enormous will-power to be able to push oneself through successive pain barriers. It's a vehicle for exploring the outer limits of human performance, where the two crews will row alongside each other until one of them decides it can no longer win – both passing University Post, the official finishing line, barely conscious.

These eight oarsmen are tuned in all the while to the shrill voice of a ninth, a coxswain, wedged like a bung in the far end of the stern. Though coxswains are usually considered a necessary evil (adding weight but not speed to the racing shell), on the Boat Race course they are imperative. Given that the Thames is a tidal river with a potentially strong current, it matters a great deal whether a crew can use this stream to their advantage or not. And this, of course, depends invariably on the skills and courage of the one who mans the rudder.

Steering aside, the stamina required to race all-out for seventeen-plus minutes (the course record, set in 1998, was 16 minutes and 19 seconds) can only be acquired gradually as the result of long and mind-numbing periods of training, over six or seven days a week, and years rather than months. And it's perhaps partly for this reason that recent Oxbridge Blues have mostly been postgraduates – greater stamina tending to come with age and experience. This maturing process began with undergraduates extending their University stint by means of a fourth year or, quite often, a research degree on some or other obscurity. This reached its apex, wrote old Oxford Blue Hugh Matheson, when Boris Rankov (of Bradford Grammar School and Corpus Christi College, Oxford) won six Blues on the trot while pondering the use of the Roman spear in 1st-century Macedonia. Fit and experienced postgraduates increasingly joined from further afield too. In the case of Americans, this was often because their own universities wouldn't allow them to continue rowing beyond their undergraduate years or because European universities were useful places to be during the Vietnam draft.[9] The race nonetheless still demonstrates (in Matheson's prose) 'for all to see the cut and thrust of the eternal rivalry between the two elite academic institutions – a rivalry known to Old Blues as the needle'.

The time it takes to cover the Championship course depends not just on physical effort or technique but, to a significant extent, on the course itself (the unpredictability of its tide may help to explain why the Boat Race continues to attract keen interest). No two consecutive tides are ever alike. And given that boats are propelled through the water by exerting pressure against it, the race is, strictly speaking, not rowed from Putney to Mortlake but over whatever piece of water happens to be flooding between these points during the race.*

---

*Take, for example, the hypothetical case where two crews rowed the course, one on the fastest possible tide, the other on the worst possible, in slow conditions of wind in the first place, in fast in the second, and suppose that both completed the distance in twenty minutes. As a matter of fact, the crew on the faster tide have driven their

Having originated in a challenge between two Harrow School boys, Charles Wordsworth of Christ Church, Oxford (son of the Master of Trinity College, Cambridge, founder of the Varsity Cricket Match in 1827, and nephew to the poet William Wordsworth), and Charles Merivale of St John's College, Cambridge (later Dean of Ely), the match is still rowed 'at or near London, each in an eight-oared boat during the Easter vacation' in full view of the public. Contemporary documents suggest that no fewer than 20,000 people travelled up to Henley to watch the very first race (which was won by Oxford). Cambridge no longer sport the original pink sashes worn around the waist in honour of their Captain, W. Snow from St. John's, but developed a preference for light blue instead – a colour that over the years acquired a distinctly mint-green hue. Some say that this was because an ageing Cambridge boatman insisted on increasing amounts of yellow being added to the light blue paint to compensate for his colour-blindness. Oxford borrowed its navy blue from Christ Church, one of its grandest colleges and known colloquially as The House, where five of its first nine athletes originated. They are still referred to as the Dark Blues. And so the battle of the Blues was born.

And what a battle it was. The rivalry between the two crews is already clear from a letter written by Wordsworth to his friend Merivale, dated 2 June 1829, or eight days before the very first Boat Race:

My dear Merivale

Thank you very much for your letter. Its impudence was unparalleled. I do not know which to admire most, its direct assertions or occult insinuations. [...] The sufficiently candid manner in which you talk of 'lasting us out' (!!!) amuses me so much, that I am ready to die with laughter whenever I

boat through only 3 miles 534 yards of water, while the crew on the slower tide will have covered 4 miles 374 yards, the exact distance of the course from the University Stone (the official starting point) to the finish. (Illustration supplied by G.C. Drinkwater in *The Boat Race* (1939).)

think of it. My dear fellow, you cannot possibly know our crew, or you would not write in such an indiscreet manner. Allow me to enlighten you:

8. Staniforth (Ch. Ch. boat): 4 feet across the shoulders and as many through the chest.

7. Moore (Ch. Ch. boat): 6 feet 1 inch; in all probability a relation of the giant whom the 'three rosy-cheeked school-boys built up on the top of Helm Crag', so renowned for length and strength of limb.

6. Garnier (Worcester boat): splendid oar.

5. Toogood (Bal. boat) – for you: but just the man for us.

4. Wordsworth (new oar): has neither words nor worth, action nor utterance, & c. I only (row) right on; I tell you that that you yourselves do know.

3. Croft (Bal. boat): no recommendation necessary.

2. Arbuthnot (Bal. boat): strong as Bliss's best.

1. Carter (St. John's four-oar): '*potentior ictu fulmineo.*'

…

Believe me,

My dear Merivale,
Sincerely yours,
C. Wordsworth

Wordsworth's letter was intended to impress. And Oxford lived up to his expectations, winning the first-ever Boat Race in 14 minutes and 30 seconds.[10]

Other than the race having moved from Henley to London, and the boats no longer being the clunky fixed-seat, fixed-pin vessels of the mid-19th century, the match today is more or less what it was on 10 June 1829: a distinctly *private* affair. For despite the public spectacle, celebrity treatment and media circus, the race remains a profound test of individual character. Away from the public eye, the athletes not only compete for a handful of seats in the coveted Blue Boat, but are forced to do battle with themselves. The Boat Race, in a sense more immediate than the fanfare that attends it, requires that rowers face up to their inner demons. To their very own *Voldemorts*. For that laborious seven-month journey towards race day is also a voyage into a mysteriously private place: into what it means to be truly and fully a man.

And so following on from Charles Wordsworth's letter, consider this year's cast.

Tom James
Born in Cardiff in 1984. 6ft 3in tall. 13st 6lbs.
Tom is the quintessential British oarsman: composed, gentlemanly and effective, but understated and modest, like a character out of a Wodehouse novel. As a fourth-year Engineering student and member of Trinity Hall, he is one of a handful of undergraduates in the squad and the only one to make this year's Blue Boat. Technically gifted, and this year's CUBC President, Tom's success on the international rowing scene is marred by three failed Boat Race attempts. The media will want to see him succeed in this, his fourth and final chance to win that prized silver trophy, or to watch him saunter into the history books as a four-time Boat Race loser. Either makes for a good story.

Kieran West, MBE
Born in Kingston upon Thames in 1977. 6ft 8in tall. 15st 6lbs.
Several years older than his President, and more highly decorated, Kieran is the tallest and oldest in the squad. Like most international oarsmen, his upper legs have bulged in response to the repeated strain of training, his calves bearing bite-marks where the boat's metal sliders have cut into the flesh. All that remains now are the familiar coffee-like stains on milky-white skin. A historian

and member of Pembroke College, Kieran is every bit the gentleman that Tom is, even if he is more assertive and also more oblivious to the effect he has on others.

Having taken home gold for Britain in the 2000 Sydney Olympics, he worries that he is nowhere near his Sydney peak. The 2004 Olympics were a disaster and, while things have improved with a fourth and fifth place in the 2005 and 2006 World Championships, Kieran is not where he wants to be performance-wise. Earlier this year both he and Tom turned down a suggestion by the GB team to shun the Boat Race and train independently in Cambridge. It was a decision that cost them dearly when their funding was subsequently withdrawn. Will their cocktail of training and full-time study cause them to be less competitive than those in the GB squad? And what will it do for their chances of a shot at the 2008 Olympics?

Peter (Pete) Champion
Born in Derby in 1982. 6ft 6in tall. 14st 11lbs.
Yet another British oarsman, though much less experienced than Kieran and Tom, Pete is at the cusp of his second attempt at making the Blue Boat. Broad-shouldered and toned, this blond and curly-haired London-trained dentist is reading psychology, hopeful of becoming 'the sort of dentist that people needn't be afraid of'. Last year he failed even to qualify as a CUBC reserve, despite having put in the same number of hours in the gym and on the water as the rest of the squad. He has spent all summer working on improving his fitness, but, unless he also improves technically, is unlikely to make the Blue Boat.

Thorsten (Tottie) Engelmann
Born in Berlin in 1981. 6ft 5in tall. 15st 7lbs.
Thorsten is easily the squad's most gentle oarsman. As CUBC's most powerful rower, and as a member of Germany's highly successful national rowing team, he is surprisingly unassuming – his modesty on a par with his dry but quiet sense of humour, all of it

accentuated by a thick German accent. Like Pete, Thorsten is a member of St Edmund's College, in pursuit of a degree in Economics.

He may have just won gold with the Deutschlandachter (the German national eight) at the World Rowing Championships at Dorney Lake, Eton, but he returns to Cambridge on the back of last year's Boat Race defeat. Besides, his financial situation is grim, forcing him to leave the house he shared with his close friend and fellow German oarsman, Sebastian Schulte, and to move back into college accommodation. Though his formidable strength and experience should warrant him a place in the Blue Boat, what he really wants is a shot at that most prestigious of seats in the boat – 'stroke' – favoured by many because it's here, in the stern of the boat, that the racing pattern is decided. But he's well aware that Kieran, too, has his eyes firmly fixed on that seat.

Sebastian (Seb) Schulte
Born in Wiesbaden in 1978. 6ft 4in tall. 14st 5lbs.
Thorsten's friend and team-mate Seb Schulte returns to Cambridge on the back of two consecutive Boat Race defeats. Like Tom, he is desperately keen to eradicate the ghastly memories of the past two races by winning his third. In terms of personality, Seb is everything Thorsten isn't: bold and assertive, unafraid, suspicious, keen to take charge of whatever situation befalls him. A member of Gonville and Caius College, he is mid-way through a PhD in Finance and Accounting at the Judge Business School, and sharp as a razor.

Having won bronze (2001 and 2005), silver (2002) and gold (2007) in the World Rowing Championships, Seb's crew just missed out on medals in the Athens Olympics. Despite a successful rowing career so far, he has yet to win his first Boat Race. This year will mark his third but also his final chance at the Boat Race trophy.

Kristopher (Kip) McDaniel
Born in Duncan, Canada, in 1982. 6ft 1in tall. 13st 6lbs.
Things hardly look better for the Canadian Kip McDaniel who, at stroke, assumed a disproportionate amount of the blame for last year's Boat Race performance. The product of a rowing family, Kip had considerable success as stroke of the Harvard boat, seeing off several Yale crews in their own version of the Boat Race. He left Cambridge, Massachusetts, for Wall Street, New York, to try his hand at financial journalism. As the work piled up, so did the pounds, and what had been a strong and muscular physique gave way rather too readily to the bulk of a New York cab-driver.

Ill-at-ease in his newly-found skin (in early 2005 Kip weighed in at 16st 1lb), he decided to try to re-enter competitive rowing, quit his job, and moved heaven and earth to return to the fitness of his undergraduate years. Despite his subsequent weight-loss, his good looks, his eloquence and natural charisma, he has a killer instinct and knows that, as one of the shortest in the squad, this land economist will have to work doubly hard to keep up with the 6ft 4in-plus likes of Kieran, Seb and Thorsten.

Daniel (Dan) O'Shaughnessy
Born in Brockville, Canada, in 1982. 6ft 2in tall. 15st 0lbs.
A fellow Canadian, Dan arrived in Cambridge overweight and unfit, hoping to join his friend Kip in the Blue Boat but unable to put down any impressive performances in training. Of a stocky build, Dan has an iridescent temperament – being at once charming and likeable, yet explosive and broody; the clown of the squad, taking neither others nor himself too seriously, yet quick to anger too.

Faced with mounting pressures at home and within the squad, things are likely to come to a head at some point during the training season. Will the natural disposition of this young land economist help or hinder his attempt at making the Blue Boat?

Jacob (Jake) Cornelius
Born in Arkansas in 1984. 6ft 6in tall. 14st 9lbs.
As one of the youngest in the squad, Jake spent four years rowing for Stanford while an Engineering undergraduate. Unlike many at Stanford, however, Jake's background is far from privileged, having grown up in upstate New York in the basement of a house built by his father. In choosing to come to Emmanuel College, Cambridge, Jake turned down an offer to train full-time with the US national squad, and unless he makes the Blue Boat, is unlikely to be welcomed back. This concern will weigh heavily on his mind as he is keen to leverage the Boat Race as preparation for his most ambitious project yet: the 2008 Beijing Olympics. However, the journey towards the Blue Boat will require him to pay a higher price than he ever imagined possible.

Russ Glenn
Born in Palo Alto in 1982. 5ft 5in tall. 8st 6lbs.
Russ Glenn, by contrast, has two Boat Race wins under his belt as coxswain of the Goldie crew (the reserve crew, Cambridge's second boat, and primary training partner for the Blue Boat). This experience should make this American former wrestler and amateur boxer a firm favourite to cox the Blue Boat – something he is desperately keen to do. Of the five triallist coxswains, the greatest threat comes from a petite but indomitable ginger-haired British woman, who will be gunning for that very same space. Will Russ's experience prevail over Rebecca's ambition?

Rebecca Dowbiggin
Born in St Albans in 1983. 5ft 6in tall. 7st 12lbs.
Having never played a sport before coming to Emmanuel College as an undergraduate four years ago, Rebecca discovered a flair for coxing. She gradually worked her way from her college boat to coxing for the Cambridge University Lightweight and Women's crews, to trialling with CUBC. She failed to get through to the last two coxswains twice previously. This will be her third time – and her determination is palpable.

So there you have it: the lead characters have arrived on stage – four Brits, two Germans, two Canadians and two Americans. They will weave in and out of the narrative but are destined to meet in the final act. And of course there are others too: Kiwi coaches Duncan Holland and Grant Craies, the Australian visiting coach Tim McLaren, and British-born Rob Baker and Donald Legget. Then there are British hopefuls Colin Scott, Marco Espin, Oli de Groot, Alistair Macleod, Doug Perrin, Tobias Garnett, David Billings, David Hopper, Richard Stutt and Pat Saunders, the Dutch Wanne Kromdijk, the German David Barst, and the brash American Don Wyper. Aside from a shared battle with themselves (against their fears and insecurities), they must do battle with each other. Over a gruelling seven months, their every stroke will be dissected, analysed, compared, and – inch-by-inch – rebuilt. For those bold enough to try for a seat in the Blue Boat can do so only by collaborating seamlessly with the very people they are competing with. They express individuality in wishing to remain on the coaches' radar screens, but togetherness in building team spirit. They are expected to adopt a rowing style that is quintessentially Cambridge, but have to learn to sacrifice what they know has made them go fast in the past. They are strong-minded yet rife with self-doubt, wise yet foolish, masculine yet unafraid of male intimacy, extraordinary in some ways yet so very ordinary in others too, ever prey to thinking that they can do always what they can do sometimes. For what makes them good makes them difficult too: they are smart, which makes them have near-perfect faith in their intuitions; they are quick thinkers, but bad listeners, prone to jump ahead in conversations, impatient and convinced they know what comes next; they are intolerant of failure, and take an extraordinary level of performance as given; will rarely admit to being wrong; and have little idea of the sort of impact their attitude has on others. Cambridge rowers are painstakingly cultivated yet remain a raw and instinctive cast of alpha males in a *Dead Poets Society* world.

This world-inside-a-world isn't all that far removed from George Orwell's 'war minus the shooting', being, like most sports, bound up with hatred, jealousy, boastfulness, disregard of all rules and sadistic pleasure in witnessing violence. How then do these flawed characters negotiate the absurdity of living with the lucid and prosaic, the narcissistic and cooperative, the youthful and nostalgic, the resistant and compliant, friend and foe?

This is mostly their story, a tale of 30 or so university students competing for just eight seats in 60 feet of yellow carbon fibre and the opportunity to see how they measure up against their arch-rivals over four miles of April water. Having lost five of the past seven Boat Races, including the last two, the stakes are unusually high. Sean Bowden, a successful coach with five Boat Race wins, would once again be coaching the Dark Blues. Cambridge's coach, by contrast, had yet to win his first. Though this crew came equipped with five returning internationals, this blessing was a mixed one. All were experienced and decorated oarsmen. Every single one had strong views on what had gone wrong in recent years and what we must now do and at all costs avoid doing – views that, needless to say, were more often than not at odds with each other. It was as Ivan Turgenev surmised: most people cannot understand how others can blow their noses differently than they do.

I realise none of this, of course, as I trade my Cambridge gown for jeans and a toggle top, and join the boys on the eve of their first day of training.

CHAPTER 4

Tuesday, 19 September 2006
(199 days to go until the 153rd Boat Race)

I take another look at my reflection in the bedroom mirror. I don't ordinarily wear ties, but then tonight's no ordinary night. In one hour's time, less even, Tom James will kick off the 2007 Boat Race campaign as President. Smitten with stock imagery from the Oxford rowing film *True Blue* (based on Daniel Topolski's account of the 1987 Oxford mutiny), I flirt with sporting my Oxford college tie, think better of it, and opt for an all-purpose variety instead.

I arrive at the appointed hour of 18:00 at Goldie: a picturesque red-brick boathouse bordering the River Cam and purpose-built in 1882 for the Cambridge University Boat Club. It's easily the proudest of a gaudy carnival of college boathouses in various architectural traditions and colours: Christ's, St John's, Queens', Peterhouse, Fitzwilliam, Trinity, St Catharine's, Trinity Hall, Jesus, Clare, Pembroke, Emmanuel, Downing, King's. These are occasionally interspersed with 'townie' rowing clubs, typically more modest and more contemporary in design. The Goldie sits trapped between St Catharine's and Jesus' boathouses, overlooking, as they do, Midsummer Common and the three-storey Victorian townhouses beyond. On the outside, facing the Cam, it features barn doors painted a Cambridge blue, and above them a balcony that stretches nearly the length of the boathouse.

Behind the balcony and immediately above the barn doors is the Captains' Room, sentimental but bedazzling to the uninitiated:

squarish with painted oak-panelled walls, a grand but impotent fireplace, wooden floorboards and dark wooden benches, light oaken chairs of various shapes and sizes and a large rectangular table, also in light oak. Cardboard coasters lie scattered about the table like slain UFOs. The panelled walls, in Cambridge blue, serve as placeholders for what may well be the Goldie's most precious asset: the names of every Boat Race crew since 1829, written prettily in gold paint on small panels, announcing merely whether that particular race was won or lost. By tradition, new names are committed to history only during successful years; thus the losing 2005 and 2006 crews won't join the pageant until Cambridge rules the Tideway once more.

The room is nearly full already when I get there, the air thick with anticipation in Cambridge's very own Ellis Island. Oak chairs stand side by side in long rows. Sitting on them are a mixture of Old Blues and Goldies, and three or so fistfuls of novices, most of whom will never see their names on the walls. Many won't survive the first three months. Following what roughly seems to be the direction of Head Coach Duncan Holland's gesturing, I sit down on one of the dark oak benches facing the crowd and am soon joined by the rest of the coaching team: Grant and Rob (aka Bakes), the tall and blonde physiotherapist Linda, and Donald, a veteran of the coaching circuit and one of the most important 'living' links between the club's past and the present day.

'So, what's your subject?' a voice hums in my right ear. It's a classic Oxbridge opening intended to size up the opposition. Should one's subject be thought frivolous, it doubles as a closing sequence.

'I'm at the business school ...' (Awkward silence.)

Tom James takes to the floor. He looks the part: handsome, black bristled hair pointing up and forward, a conspicuously long, thin face and correspondingly thin-rigged nose slightly hooked, dark deep-set eyes that droop at the outer corners, strong chin, fair skin, a bad shave. He wears the traditional Blues blazer and Hawks tie, but seems somewhat ill at ease, as if not used to addressing large gatherings. The Welsh son of a dapper soldier, he's been blessed with extraordinary athletic talent – for rowing, for football, for rugby, for track and field, for tennis – so much so, in fact, that the challenge was always that of choosing which sport to take seriously. Even as early as his very first day at school, Tom knew he'd be fastest on the running track and so he bloody well made sure he was. Ever since, things seem to have come easily: the Cambridge degree, a world bronze medal at the tender age of twenty, captaincy of King's School Chester Boat Club before that, and now President of one of the grandest student clubs in the world. Then there's the beautiful blonde who chased him instead of he her, and a highly structured routine to his every day of every week of every month and season, leaving him with little to get worked up about except, of course, that damned affair between Putney and Mortlake.

Tom came desperately close in 2003 when separated on the finish line from Oxford by scarcely a foot. It was to be the closest-ever Boat Race result in a string of 149. As Boat Race chronicler G.C. Drinkwater points out, more often than not (at least prior to 1939), the race was a 'mere procession, with one crew far ahead rowing in perfect style well within themselves, and the other scrambling along, broken in heart and mind, a beaten crew, far behind.' Having lost again in 2005 and for a third time the follow-ing year by a dispiriting five lengths, he is yet to master that singu-lar feat: winning the Boat Race. That's what tonight is about. Tonight there is no room for self-doubt.

Tonight he is God.

The Captains' Room with its gold-lettered panelling pretty much encapsulates what the Club is about, Tom tells an attentive audience. The Club exists for one reason alone: to beat Oxford in the annual Boat Race. To lose the race means to consign an entire year to the dust heap, joining the 72 lost years already there. (Inci-dentally, there has only ever been one draw in Boat Race history. In 1877, the umpire John Phelps declared the result a dead-heat to Oxford by 5 feet.)

Looking at Tom, I can't help but feel sympathy towards this 22-

year-old weighed down by the yoke of three defeats and now standing at the launch of this, his fourth attempt. He knows, as do friends, journalists, television reporters, as does everyone, that it's now or never. Boris Rankov had that one sorted out. After his sixth successive Boat Race, the two universities drew up a Memorandum of Understanding that limited the number of races for individual oarsmen: 'a student may only row in four Boat Races as an undergraduate and four Boat Races as a graduate, i.e. the maximum number of Boat Races in which any single student may compete is eight.'

To be President, particularly against the backdrop of three personal losses, is no easy task. It remains one of the most prestigious student-held posts in the University and allows those elected to leave their fingerprints on the future course of Cambridge rowing. Such was the case, for instance, with Joe Fraser (CUBC President in 1964–65) who went on to introduce the now-familiar Goldie–Isis race, allowing Cambridge and Oxford's reserve boats to race the course some 30 minutes prior to their Blue Boats. Joe's was an unusually impressive achievement, seeing that he had just lost his father, mother and brother in a freak hurricane which caused their yacht to capsize en route to Jersey.

The CUBC Presidency has sometimes been described as akin to being in charge of a large corporation, sitting on a handful of committees and responsible for all strategic decisions, yet spending most of one's time on the shop floor. It has always required modesty as well as responsibility. For example, should the fastest crew on 7 April not include Tom yet still be the fastest crew, he will have succeeded in his office. The constitutional position of a President is, after all, that of selecting the fastest possible crew to race Oxford. But it also entails such other things as chairing the Blues Committee, commissioned with awarding sporting Blues to University sportsmen and women – a full Blue being the highest sporting honour bestowed on any Oxbridge student.

Cambridge's distinctive blue seems to have originated in the second-ever Boat Race in 1836. It's said that just before the race,

R.N. Phillips of Eton and Christ's College suggested that Cambridge should have a colour at its bows, called at a haberdashers and asked for a piece of ribbon or silk. The colour happened to be light blue, possibly because it was Eton's colour or that of Gonville and Caius College (there were three Caians in the boat), or maybe because it was simply the nearest bit of ribbon to hand. Cambridge adopted the colour the next year in its race against the metropolitan rowing club Leander (Oxford refused Cambridge's invitation to a race in 1837 and 1838, and so Cambridge challenged Leander instead). At the very least, this makes for a believable alternative to our colour-blind boatman.

The audience in the Captains' Room has gone eerily silent. One or two shuffle around in an effort to get more comfortable on the hard wooden chairs. Kieran, legs stretched, sits staring at his size 13 shoes. Kip, hands folded in his lap, looks down and sideways, the wounds of his recent defeat still raw. It was he, after all, who had controversially been placed in the stroke seat at the last minute, trying his best to keep rhythm through the rough Tideway waters but forced to admit defeat at last as the boat took on water and the rowing became unbearable. Oxford, like the five judicious virgins of the Gospel of St Matthew, came prepared. Armed with pumps, they won by a humiliating five lengths.

The pumps-or-no-pumps debate continued for some time after the race had been decided, Cambridge mocked for its decision not to install them. In some ways it was an interesting reversal of 1987, when Oxford's coach Daniel Topolski noticed with 'a degree of satisfaction' that Cambridge had installed an electric pump whereas Oxford had not, but that his crew were coping much better with the rough water conditions. Then again, as both Topolski and his President Barney Williams put it after the 2006 race, the pumps weren't even used. Oxford, they say, were simply better in rough water and Cambridge didn't take on nearly as much water as they claim ('I saw them empty their boat out at the finish and it wasn't that full,' the former Oxford coach would say later).

Not until Cambridge's controversial choice to enter the Head of the River Race with only seven days to go until the 2007 Boat Race, under the same appalling weather conditions as in 2006 but armed with battery-operated pumps, were the boys finally able to appease the demons of that ghastly affair – a useful reminder that the wind and the tide never cease to bedevil. The outcome of the race can be heavily influenced by the weather, the power of the tide, or the coin toss that decides which side of the river is theirs to race on.

'The reason we lost in '06 was because we were stopped dead by the heavy waves on the Middlesex station at Chiswick Eyot, then nearly sank as we took on loads of water, while Oxford took on none because they were on Surrey, so were able to steer out of this rough water while forcing us to stay in it,' Kieran tells me, clearly agitated. 'Though with the people we had on board we should have been able to win the race by Hammersmith, been clear ahead of Oxford, and sheltered on the Surrey station before getting to the point where the weather on Middlesex became as critical as it did. This year we've got to get the crew to settle into a rhythm in a way we were never able to achieve last year.' To achieve this – to gel the crew into a human franchise with one mind and one rhythm – will be this year's single most important objective.

Wednesday, 20 September

I arrive at Goldie a few minutes before eight and in good time for the first set of erg tests. The boathouse is teeming with triallists, some stretching, others warming up on Concept II rowing ergometers. This ergometer (or 'erg' for short) is a modern-day rowing machine that allows oarsmen to exercise their muscles and measure their output in the comfort of a heated gym. It features a large fly-wheel, a moving seat, and a small digital display. Those who have warmed up already pace the gym, ears pulsating with hip-hop and disco fed through tiny earplugs, their worked-up sweat trickling in droplets onto the rubbery floor, tracing their every move.

I, meanwhile, meander about tentatively, notepad and pen in hand, like a fish out of water. After all, they don't know me and I don't know them.

The tests take place in a new extension to The Goldie boat-house. Though architecturally in a different league as far as the outside is concerned, on the inside it features the same green rubber floors and plastered white walls. On these walls rowing machines are strung up, 29 in all, like Christmas turkeys in cold storage. The weightlifting equipment, dated and rudimentary, has been stockpiled into the far end of the old section, to be used twice weekly. Large wood-framed mirrors on wheels stand scattered around the two rooms, waiting expectantly and reflecting the soulless fluorescent tubes bolted to the white ceiling. Posters of different shapes and sizes, mostly souvenirs of battles fought and won, are Blu-Tacked to the walls. One of these features a pretty, scantily-dressed red-head flaunting a burgundy bra, lips slightly apart, a corner of the print torn off and now flopping forward. Like some others, it will have peeled off and been reattached many a time.

There is a door ajar at the back, and behind it a mirrored room and water tank for indoor technical coaching. The size of a small pool, it consists of a blue tub with seats and oars attached to it, allowing athletes to strap in and practise their technique in the water without ever leaving the boathouse. The room is apparently also used as a de facto storage space, with several bikes flung casually in a heap.

At Duncan's command, the triallists push away from their foot-plates, their first full strokes slow but the pace picking up rapidly until settling at a rating of about 34 strokes a minute. As they increase this rating, their splits take a nosedive. (A split is a standard measurement in rowing and represents the time it takes to row a distance of 500 metres.) The stronger and more experienced rowers are able to maintain a split somewhere close to 1:30 (or 1 min 30 secs) per 500 metres – or at least for the first 1,200 to 1,500 metres. In the last third of the 2,000-metre stretch, the performance of most rapidly turns south, as their current fitness level doesn't allow them to sustain this sort of speed. It will soon.

The Cambridge training programme is designed to build endurance through long erg sessions in the morning (up to 80 minutes) and even longer, three-quarter pressure but relatively low-rating outings on the River Great Ouse, in Ely, in the afternoons and on weekends. It's a physically punishing schedule.

As the guys pull away on the ergs, the coaches wander about the gym looking at such things as posture, style, and split times, hoping to get some idea of the consistency by which power is applied as well as the extent of its deterioration. In the background Madonna's 'Hung Up' is spewed from cheap plastic speakers wired to an iPod, the volume cranked up too high for its own good, garbling the output. No one cares.

As the first batch of triallists are punishing their lungs and legs on the ergs, those yet to be tested loiter behind them, showing increasing interest as the 2,000-metre mark comes in sight. They stand hunched over, peering at the small computer displays to read off the relevant data: current splits, average split times, distances remaining, strokes per minute – all of it feeding that competitive, very primal animal spirit. After the first batch is done, they'll have thrown down the gauntlet. They will have set the standard for those yet to erg – a suite of figures that, as everyone well knows, is a first attempt at ranking the triallists. This ranking, crude to start with, will gradually be refined as new batches rise to the occasion this morning, and to the many tests yet to come.

By lunchtime, all have peeled off their ergs and headed for their colleges for a late breakfast. The coaches meanwhile have retired to the upstairs Coaches' Room to jointly chew over this first set of results. Not quite sure what to do, I slip inside and grab a chair. Duncan is busy entering the morning's results on his old, stickered-up laptop. Donald sits hunched over a desktop at the far end of the room; Linda, next to Donald, works her way through a stack of typed sheets of paper, wetting her middle finger every so often as she flicks through the pages. Bakes and Grant haven't yet arrived. Bakes is responsible for training the Goldie crew, Grant for the Dev (or Development) squad and the spare pair – those not good enough to make the cut but single-minded enough nonetheless to stick around.

The room itself is disorderly: four desks of different shapes and sizes, three generations of computers, a photocopier, a sink with dishes, spoons, mugs, used teabags and goodness knows what else inside it, a dwarf fridge, a pair of metal lockers jammed open and now beyond repair, five chairs of different ancestry. A long bookshelf some ten feet up is cluttered with trophies won by generations of oarsmen, untouched, it seems, since won and now accumulating thick layers of dust, like fur. The stained blue carpet is obscured by boxes, discarded sheets of paper, old newspapers, running shoes untied but used quite recently, blue plastic crates stuffed with other trophies as if they were of no importance. Looking at this silverware carelessly lined up on windowsills, shelves, desks, in boxes, on the floor, it dawns on me that winning here is the norm. It would be unusual not to.

The other boathouse in Ely, twelve miles north of Cambridge, is much less striking, the bastard offspring of an aeroplane hangar and a seaside lavatory. Gone are the trophies and pretty panelling and wooden floorboards. The boatshed is more or less exactly that – a modest affair with a tin corrugated roof, large barn doors facing the river and a concrete dock separating water from mortar. Inside it are a changing room with painted concrete floors and white walls, a shower cubicle with six generous shower heads, a toilet block with porcelain bogs and a couple of urinals so close together that two cannot pee without touching. Neither space nor privacy is a priority here. Then there's a crew room carpeted in a worn and sweat-soaked pink, with a TV and video unit, a solitary ergometer, and a couple of veneered tables that are cheap without being cheerful, under windows facing the river.

The bulk of the boathouse is designed to store boats: five or so singles – three of which are strung up from the broad iron beam supporting the sloping corrugated roof – eight pairs, six fours and three eights, one of which will be used to race Oxford come April. All lie as if dead on wooden racks. Underneath them is an assembly of spare parts, tools, trestles, outboard engines for the coaching launches, and various colourful bits and bobs, everything having some relevance no doubt to the task at hand.

I join Donald on one of the white plastic catamarans used as coaching launches. Each features a small bench, broad enough for two adults. Any overflow of guests, coaches or spares are assigned to the Tin Fish – a flat-bottomed silvery dustpan five feet wide and twice as long, and the bane of rowers, given the enormous wake generated by its big, flat, square rear end. Donald, himself an Old Blue who rowed the Boat Race in 1963 and 1964, losing the first, winning the second, has been coaching Cambridge since 1968. Originally for only two weeks a season, as was the convention before the arrival of professional coaches in the mid-80s, Old Blues would take turns returning to their university (usually taking two weeks off work) to do a stint of coaching before handing the reins to a finishing coach for the final three weeks of Boat Race preparation.

Donald remains the club's most important connection to the past, having been part of the coaching team for 40 years. Aside from his skills as a coach, his link to a bygone age and deep-seated passion for Cambridge rowing make the crew feel part of something bigger, and give them that all-important sense of place. Today, Donald's light-grey windblown locks accentuate that unmistakeable British countryside tinge on nose and cheeks.

'Be great to have my knees replaced,' he grumbles as he painfully hobbles from the boatshed across the concrete to the catamaran, 'but that takes time, and time is something I don't have a lot of.' He wheezes as he heaves his bulk into the white plastic and onto an inflatable rubber pillow. And so we the happy pair take off lopsided, uncertain of what else, if anything, to say to each other.

Whatever Donald's knees fail to provide, his eyes more than make up for. As I watch him in action – light-blue fleece vest and dark-blue fleece trousers, two stopwatches around his thick neck, one silver, one red, his matted unkempt hair held in place by a baseball cap, an old battery-operated megaphone in one hand, steering wheel in the other – I am amazed at his ability to pick up even the smallest of nuances in rowing. He easily spots subtle differences in style, in set-up (or rigging) and blade work, and is able to make calls that, however trivial in appearance, have a marked effect on boat speed. For underneath that surly veneer lives a bloody good rowing coach with a superb eye and sense of rhythm.

At Goldie, meanwhile, Jake Cornelius has arrived. A tanned, ashen-haired Stanford oarsman just back from a stint of volunteer work as a mechanical engineer with the rural poor in El Salvador, he once completed 2000m on the erg in 5 mins 55 secs, a very fast time. Everyone seems very hopeful of him making the Blue Boat. But of course they don't know yet, do they?

CHAPTER 5

As a variation on the usual, Duncan orders half the boys onto bikes for a semi-strenuous ride while the others stay put to work their core muscles. These muscles, located mostly in the lower back and abdomen, help ensure good control over movements in the boat. Cycling, on the other hand, works the leg muscles but without putting too heavy a strain on the back. I borrow a rusty old bike from Dan, once no doubt a fashionable hybrid but in its present incarnation well beyond its sell-by date, and join the athletes. As we pedal away from Goldie and out of Cambridge I am thrilled to find myself keeping up. The riding isn't nearly as hard as I'd imagined. I'm not doing too badly, frankly, being only second-to-last in the line-up, and with power to spare speed proudly along, my head held high. It never occurs to me that we're merely cycling to the start of our circuit.

I'm pooped by the time we reach the starting point: the gated entrance of Impington's swimming pool, the hub of a small village on Cambridge's outskirts. The brash and tough Dartmouth oarsman Don Wyper takes the lead and explains our route:

'Turn left at the end of this road, then halfway down that road turn around and head back, and continue going straight past this road for about one mile and a half, then turn around and come back this way to the swimming pool, and then do the same thing again – see y'all later.'

Self-assured, the American mounts his anorexic aluminium horse, clicks his shoes onto sawn-off pedals, tucks his wild dark-brown locks underneath a flash carbon helmet, and, caring not whether anyone understood his instructions, speeds off. Typical Don, still resentful at not having made the Blue Boat last year. I suddenly feel distinctly out of place in baggy khakis, T-shirt, hot feet and mud-stained running shoes, the euphoria of a moment ago all but vanished.

Never having been quick at grasping instructions, I nonetheless batter away noisily to the music of dry ball bearings, as my knackered pushbike and I give chase. In no time I'm wheezing like a hoover. My legs are burning painfully. I pedal as fast as I can, and yet the distance between the boys and me is growing. I'm thrusting the pedals as if my life depended on it – or if not my life, my credibility – my legs moving fast enough now to bring it up a gear, except that I can't figure out how to use the offending contraption. Flicking switches left and right seems to make no difference whatsoever – the bicycle chain steadfastly holding to the excessively worn treads of too small a gear. And so I spend the first half of the outing pedalling at what feels like several hundred revolutions per minute. Before long, I'm nauseous – my lower back is aching badly and I'm considering cutting corners by not cycling the second lap, or turning back earlier than the rest. I'm so far behind now, they would never know. But I would, of course, which is worse.

I'm sweat-soaked and unable to speak by the time I complete both laps and arrive back at the village pool. The boys look at me curiously.

'Gonna do the triathlon this weekend?' Don smirks. Eighteen pairs of eyes glance at me from underneath carbon headgear.

'Fuck no—'

I can barely speak for lack of oxygen. Salty drops of sweat trickle down and sting my eyes. I blink and squint, half-hoping the boys will think me tough but suspecting they'll see through the charade. As Duncan proudly announced this morning, the conclusion of the two-week boot camp will be marked by a mini-triathlon, intended as another stab at ranking the athletes and fuelling competition between them. After all, there are places for only eight rowers and one coxswain in the Blue Boat – in the only boat that, harsh though it sounds, matters.

CHAPTER 6

'Did you know that I used to cox for my local police force?' We are standing in the cramped changing room at Ely, looking nonplussed at this novice coxswain.

'Back in County Durham, you know …'

The boys are swapping stories in an attempt at breaking the ice and showing that, under that veneer of Oxbridge privilege, one is and remains a man like any other, with a beating heart and lustful thoughts.

'Well, anyway, after rainy outings the lads would dry their gear in the club dryer. See, we didn't have a washing machine but we did have a dryer. Now one of them had caught crabs but hadn't told anyone, or maybe he didn't even know himself, who knows …'

(What on earth are *crabs*?)

'And so here he goes throwing his all-in-one in with the rest of their stuff … in the dryer where it's nice and warm, right? Now imagine this, a few days later, five of them had the damn things. You can imagine how they'd explain that to their wives—'

He cackles. Jake farts hoarsely.

This being a changing room, there's bound to be changing room talk – one of relatively few corners where class distinctions matter little, or seem to anyway. It's stuff like this that provides that much-needed lifting of the gloom, anxiety and apprehensiveness, the camaraderie and spite forced to cohabit in that same cramped space – a movable feast of complex emotions that one joins but can never leave. The Canadian international and Cambridge Blue Kip McDaniel gives a nice example of this in his internet blog. He reflects on his training with the Canadian squad before stepping onto the Cambridge-bound plane:

PRIMAL INTENTIONS

By: Kip McDaniel

Rowing at this level brings out the most base emotions and primal intentions. When you're rowing with the national team, you're always – and I mean always – looking out for your own self-interest.

A good example of this happened today in the Canadian camp. This morning, one of our three heavyweight sweep boats was doing some selection. Not being in this boat, I had very little interest in the result – or so it seemed. With one port side oar challenging another for his seat in this boat, tensions were high and racing was intense. The challenger, who arrived in camp after this boat had been provisionally set, wanted a shot at a seat, and the coach gave it to him.

The loser of this challenge would come into the boat I am currently in. The person being challenged was a good friend of mine, one who I had rowed with at last year's world championships. I respect his work ethic and speed, and only hoped the best for him in his time trial.

Here's where the primal intentions come in, however. Because I like him, and because I trust him wholeheartedly in any race situation, I want him in my boat. On one level – a higher one, in a moral framework – I wanted him to win the time trial, because no one likes to fail. However, on another level, I wanted him to lose, because I know he would be a unifying force in my boat and would add to the lightheartedness that we have now and certainly had last year in our boat. He's a fun guy to row with and he's fast, and because of this, I was hoping he would be joining us.

In the end, this friend lost the time trial by the smallest of margins, and will be joining us. On one level, I am sad for him, because he had been in that boat for months and was expecting to be in it for London. However, on a more primal level – and ultimately the one that matters in international rowing – I wanted him in my boat. My wishes won out over his, and I am frankly happy. That's the way competing at this level goes. So be it.

Ironically, the forces that generate such uncomfortable emotions – cooperation and competition (where the latter is only ever achieved by means of the former), trust and vigilance, empathy and assertiveness, confrontation and compromise, justice and mercy, affection and exploitation, the routine and the unexpected, abstinence and profligacy, the sacred and the profane – not only coexist but must do so. Fast, effective rowing relies on collaboration, yet competition keeps the fire at the feet of those trialling, squeezing out every last bit of performance. This strategy of postponing final selection until the last possible moment is not without risks, however. Crews can peak too early, or not at all, if too little time is left for them to learn to work together as a unit. Or, as Donald likes to point out, competitive pressures can make nonsense of the form book, never more so than in the famous mutiny race of 1987, when an Oxford crew surrounded by weeks of acrimony and dispute and without several of their star oarsmen beat a Cambridge boat expected by most pundits to carry it off.[11]

These tensions cannot be straightforwardly resolved. But one can learn to live with them. One resource for coping is humour, and (as any comedian will tell you) humour is most easily and cheaply had by exploiting that lowest common denominator, allowing one to tell those around him that underneath it all we are so very much alike. So very much like ordinary men.

Likewise, the boys oscillate between rowing and studying – their acceptance into the University being contingent upon academic merit alone. Coxswains need to be able to understand at any point in a race what the crew are still capable of doing physiologically and yet be assertive enough to make bold and risky calls and take responsibility for them. Such might be the case when, for instance, a mighty push of fifteen powerful strokes could 'break' an opponent – a call that can only realistically be made once or twice during a seventeen-minute race. Crew selection entails a fair amount of science, spending hours poring over seat-racing results, pairs' matrices, erg test results, race performances. And yet so much of what coaches do is intuitive too, particularly when it comes to finding the right combination of oarsmen. Crew selection is not and never can be a mere matter of totting up individual erg scores and isolating the eight strongest rowers, handing them a coxswain, a boat and eight blades, and setting them off. Were it that simple, a computer program could decide crew selection and do away with countless hours spent in heated meetings analysing endless reams of data, soliciting subjective assessments of who looks good in what seat and who works well with whom.

What makes selection tricky, at least in part, is that rowers can perform differently depending on who else is in the crew. Oarsmen like to row with oarsmen they respect, where respect is earned the hard way by putting in the miles and bringing home the medals. Occasionally even, pride will prevent them from performing optimally if they are assigned any seat other than those they think are 'theirs' by right, often somewhere in the stern of the boat, a place viewed as among the more prestigious and responsible. This poses a particular problem for coaches: namely whether it's better to cater to egos in the interest of boat speed, or to suppress them in the interest of fairness and equality. It's a problem to which the solution is far from obvious.

To dwell in this world of irreconcilable trade-offs, where one thing is invariably achieved at the expense of something else, to achieve but at a cost – it is the acquiescence to this that makes their world different from ours. And I suspect it's here too that laddishness plays a decisive role in making this world more habitable. Where tensions are impossible to reconcile, humour, even if cheaply had, can work miracles. What you can't cry about, you can try to laugh about; and what you can laugh about, you can face up to.

In much the same way, intimacy may help arbitrate where words fail, telling others that they're really okay, that this is nothing personal, that competition is forced upon them by virtue of the situation, that it's business as usual – and why not shake on it?

'There's a solution to crabs, however,' our novice coxswain continues. 'You take a scorching hot shower and then rub alcohol on it.'

I can do with some fresh air at this stage and join Boris, another trialling coxswain, on the concrete dock outside. Tied to it are the two white coaching catamarans; facing them on the concrete, the Tin Fish lies like a stripped, discarded tin of sardines.

I try to make conversation. 'What's up?'

Boris seems less than thrilled by the crew line-up for today. Boris, like Nick, Russ and Rebecca, is here to trial as a coxswain, and like them he is a good foot or so shorter than the oarsmen. He is by far the heaviest of the foursome, or looks it, which is unlikely to curry him favour with the boys. Looking at him now, I can't help but find him somewhat uninspiring – self-pitying, mawkish, bitter – exhibiting none of the characteristics that crews thrive on, like buoyancy, poise, level-headedness; that, and a sense of rhythm.

'I'm with you in the tin fucking fish!'

'That'll be nice.'

'It's not fucking *nice* – I should be in one of the eights.'

I state the obvious. There are too many coxswains and too few coxed boats, and so you're bound to be rotated in and out. What's so unique about that?

'It's just that Russ and Rebecca have had twice as many outings as I have.'

'They have, have they?'

'They've had four each so far and I've only been out twice, meaning the coaches have either already made their selection and decided I'm out, in which case there's no point me hanging around here, or decided I'm fine, but they want to have another look at the others.'

In his dreams. I doubt he'll last the week. No way he's got what it takes.

CHAPTER 7

Talking of dreams, last night I found myself standing like Brezhnev's generals in a bog surrounded by urinals and plastic partitions, my cubicle oddly positioned in the middle of what was a surprisingly small lavatory – the whole place exceedingly dirty and saturated with piss, my feet inch-deep in the stuff and the porcelain crusted with sediments of human waste, and inside it crumpled up tissue. And so I do what most do under the circumstances when prodded by Mother Nature and unable to hold it much longer: look for toilet tissue to cover up the dirty bits and create a makeshift stool.[12]

As luck would have it, I notice a nearly-full roll. But before I have the chance to uncoil it, I drop the roll accidentally on the tiled floor and into the puddle of piss. There is no fucking way I can use this paper now. And then, as I'm considering my options, colleagues come walking into my small cubicle which I hadn't realised wasn't actually locked, and so we stand there awkwardly shoulder to shoulder with nothing much to say but me desperate for relief …

I wake up to the ring tone of my Motorola, confused, more in my dream than out of it. Wasn't it C.S. Lewis who wrote that dreams don't suddenly disappear when unmasked for the delusions they are? They are unmistakably different from waking moments and yet somehow related to them. They are what links our being awake and our being asleep in such a way that the former is permanently and from time to time decisively changed by the latter.

'Just leaving home,' croaks Martin at the other end of the line.

I close my Motorola and, as best I can, read the numbers off its illuminated blue display: 5:30am. I sit up on the edge of my bed, having left my head elsewhere, or so it seems. I'm not feeling too good this morning.

Martin's call is my cue. Time to get on track for Boston's Head of the River Charles Regatta, the largest of its kind. Today, however, I won't be travelling with the Cambridge squad but with a town crew instead – a City of Cambridge Rowing Club Four composed of Mary (our coxswain), Martin (at stroke), Barney, me, and James, in that order. Martin has found us some sponsorship money to help pay for the transatlantic flight and related expenses. Having rowed our own race, I'll catch up with the CUBC to see them off for theirs. Cambridge has a genuine shot at the Headship this year, having ended in second place in 2005 behind Princeton. The Regatta is one of a small handful of key events in the training calendar, the others being Birmingham's Indoor Rowing Championship, the EON Hanse Cup in Germany, Fairbairns (a lock-to-lock race on the River Cam), and London's Head of the River Fours, Trial Eights, and two fixtures (mock races against internationally competitive crews). All these provide valuable selection data and allow the coaches to experiment with different combinations of oarsmen.

I stuff some quickly prepared sandwiches in my rucksack and head out into the dark and chilly morning. Ahead lies Maid's Causeway. At any other time of day, this would have been one of Cambridge's busiest thoroughfares. It now lies calm and deserted. A breeze rustles the leaves on the trees overhead. A lamp post purrs contentedly. After all the fuss of getting ready, I'm enjoying this rare lull, and feel surprisingly relaxed. Still drowsy from a late night, yet refreshed too by the wintry morning air, I reach for my toes, keeping my legs straight all the while, to stretch my hamstrings. Then, straightening up and facing heavenward, point my fingers at the stars. The sensation of pulling at my abdominal muscles is pleasurable. I reach a little further still, the effort pulling the shirt out of my trousers. The cold air grabs hold of my exposed stomach almost immediately.

Using my hand as a spade, I crumple its tails back into my khakis. In the distance, to my left, I make out the blue-hued headlights of Martin's beemer. He drives aggressively, he always does, his tyres voicing disapproval as he brakes abruptly then pulls into our narrow street, stops, and reverses back out into the Causeway and onto the pavement.

'Let's go!' says Martin.

'What about Mary and James and Barney?'

'We'll pick her and James up on the way. Barney's meeting us at Heathrow.'

I peer into the boot of his car. 'What's in that grey tube?'

'That's Barney's, that is. It's his yard-of-ale glass. Said he wanted to bring it along for after the race and asked if he could drop it off at my house seeing that he had a party in London last night and is staying at his dad's. Made that himself, he did. Duct-taped a shit-load of styrofoam together. Took him quite a while too.'

How Barney. He's so damn proud of that glass, carting it from one post-race party to the next. Drinking and rowing have long been bedfellows, Barney and his yard-of-ale glass good exemplars of this kinship. The glass itself resembles a yard-long test-tube with a bulbous head and skinny middle. If drunk properly, three pints can be downed in one go by rotating the glass as it releases the liquid inside.

At Heathrow, we must look as if caught in a time-warp: decked out in tacky blue-and-burgundy polyester blazers flaring out at the hips, club crest on the breast pocket, matched all the while by a polyester club tie, thin, short, and curling upwards. Having got used to hanging around with the Cambridge squad, I feel distinctly self-conscious, like a boy about to embark on a school trip.

The flight itself is uneventful. Once across the pond, we swap into jeans and T-shirts and head out in search of our first pint of Bostonian beer. It's not even gone two in the afternoon, and I've not had anything to eat since leaving England nine hours ago. But beer it is, in Boston's original Cheers bar, no less.

'Here we are, lads!' says Martin proudly.

'I could do with something to eat actually,' I mumble in reply. 'I'm bloody starving.'

'Should have had your lunch on the aeroplane then, shouldn't you?' scoffs Martin.

I don't bother telling him I didn't fancy the aeroplane food, seeing that he wolfed down his. Persuaded that the pub might well conjure up some sandwiches if asked, we make our way down the familiar steps and order five pints of Sam Adams Seasonal and a generous serving of nachos and quesadillas. After these five we order five more.

> WOODY BOYD: Pour you a beer, Mr Peterson?
> NORM PETERSON: All right, but stop me at one. Make that one-thirty.*

I feel dizzy.

We meander over to the city's North Side in search of something more substantial than nachos. Stacking up on carbohydrates seems like a decent plan to all, and there's plenty of that to be had in Boston's 'Little Italy'. We scour various menus from the pavement outside and decide on an Italian, as much for the smell as for the menu: of home-cooked fare, prosciutto, salami, cheese, waxed wooden wine-stained floorboards, musty brick and mortar. We chat about tomorrow's race, the world's largest, attracting some 8,000 rowers to 55 different events over two full days. First held in October 1965, the race was established by three Cambridge University Boat Club members, with the aim of staging an event similar to that on the Thames. As a 'head race', the three-mile course pits boats against each other and the clock, with crews starting at fifteen-second intervals. Winners of the various races receive the honorary title of Head of the Charles which, unsurprisingly, is an honour unlikely ever to be bestowed on us. Not that this dissuades us from partaking.

*From the TV show *Cheers*.

Friday, 20 October

I share a room with James, a Cambridge-educated materials scientist. Skinny but muscular, 5ft 8in tall, blond curly hair and blue eyes, he has his own reasons for being here. His girlfriend rows with the Cambridge University Women's Boat Club and our expedition abroad is a mere excuse for seeing more of her. She stays with her crew in a hotel across town. Our own room is small and spartan, possibly part of what was once a student dormitory – which wouldn't be surprising in a city with over 30 different universities. My suspicions are reinforced when examining the bathroom facilities. The shower consists of a metal pipe without a shower head, though there's something inside the pipe that's meant to interfere with the water flow. The pipe wheezes water along at considerable speed and in spurts. It's painful, like being blasted with sand, and entering the shower front-first is ill-advised, as James, nursing his foreskin, discovered.

After showers and lunch we are off en route to the legendary Charles River. There we will take receipt of our borrowed American-made Vespoli. It's a far older boat than any of us had imagined, soft and pliable, all 45 feet of it. There's no way we're going to pick up any speed in this thing. Much of our power will simply be absorbed by the shell, like energy invested in pushing a rubber band forwards along a rough surface. This is why Oxford and Cambridge keep their boats for no more than two, or at most three, seasons. Stiffness in rowing means speed.

We take turns poking fun at the scrounged shell before settling down to rig it. I dig into my rucksack for tools, only to realise that our metric tools are useless in this imperial world. And so we stand around awkwardly with useless bits of equipment in hand until the driver of our trailer comes over, wondering whether we might like to use some of his. He hands us a pitch gauge. It looks nothing like the gauges we're used to.

'How the fuck does this thing work?' whispers Martin. 'We're going to look like complete bollocks, aren't we, if we can't even figure out how to work this thing.'

We try several variations and ultimately make do with one that gives us a set of readings that seem workable – or at least allow us to get consistent heights and pitches throughout the boat. We rig the boat.

Then we row the three-mile course.

Saturday, 21 October

I have been awake since four. So has James. We linger on under our worn woollen blankets to shelter from the cool breeze drifting in through the open bedroom window. The sky is a cloudless blue. Both James and I are pondering today's Head of the Charles race. Little wonder really that we can't get back to sleep. To imagine some 8,000 oarsmen plagued by similar anxieties is a sobering thought.

We get dressed and head a few doors down to Billy's Coffee Shop, a local outfit recommended by our hotel clerk. Its simple menu is carved in great black letters on a brightly-lit white panel above the counter, prices in red, no pictures. Famished, we each grab a plastic chair around one of the yellow and red chequered tables, peering all the while at the illuminated menu.

'I want a fry-up,' says Martin. 'I'm fucking starving.'

'Fry-up' is something the waitress isn't familiar with, and so Martin deconstructs the order into pork sausages, bacon strips, fried eggs, fried tomatoes if they have any, and a short stack of pancakes with maple syrup – and that'll be all, ta.

'Must be hungry,' she replies softly, her ballpoint pen scurrying across a makeshift notepad. The fluorescent ceiling lights are bright, too bright for this hour, and I squint as I work out what's on offer.

'And what can I do for you honey?'

'I'll have some pancakes too, please, and eggs, and some hash-browns, please, thank you,' I say.

Despite our hunger, we're unable to finish our breakfasts. We're far too nervous. Tired of playing with our food, we grab our kit and taxi out to the river, get our Vespoli on the water and paddle the two-odd miles to the start of the race. There we're told that we're an hour early and could we please find somewhere to dock? Three-quarters of an hour later, we're finally allowed to assume a starting position, and eighteen minutes after that we're in the chute and racing.

The boat feels heavy. Our catches and our finishes aren't synchronised, and with the same amount of effort but better coordination the boat could be moving a hell of a lot faster. I half hope that none of the Cambridge squad are watching from the riverbank. My hamstrings are hurting, as is my lower back, and I'm not able to get a good hold of the water. Even so, we manage to hold off a much younger and fitter crew for half a mile before surrendering to their superior rhythm. In many ways, this feels like the best part of the race. Our coxswain calls for ten power strokes.

'Ten strokes on the knees – and push and hold – and push and hold – and push and hold – swing – swing—'

I'm gasping for air and try to focus on stabilising my breathing. To let go of some of the power is so very tempting – everything hurts, everything feels miserable. I feel sick as Mary calls for another ten power strokes, the air clumped high up in my throat, the taste of blood on my tongue.

'In two – in one – and ten – and nine – and eight – and seven – push the knees down – six – and five—'

I badly want to let go of the oar and leave this bloody river, to know it's all over and not care one iota, and would have gladly done so except that finishing a race knowing that you haven't really given it all, that you have something left in the kitty, that you could have pushed harder, is worse – immeasurably worse – than the pain and agony I now feel. As any oarsman will tell you, there's nothing worse, nothing more humiliating and more sickening, than seeing your crew mates fallen over with exhaustion and yet feeling that you could have pushed harder. All that remains is for you to live with the guilt, knowing that you let your side down. That sort of mental anguish lingers, as opposed to the sheer physical discomfort of racing, which is over as soon as you've crossed the finish line. O glorious finish line – where the hell art thou? And so I push as hard as I can, filling my blade as best I can in the choppy Charles River. We still haven't been able to find a good rhythm and negotiate a truce with our borrowed shell, and the rowing remains heavy throughout.

We're now three-quarters through the race. I feel light-headed, short of breath, legs sapped of strength, lower back in flames, yet trying desperately to stay focused on technique – on trying to make the row easier, lighter, by letting the boat do more of the work. But as in so many races, having expended so much energy already by this point on the course, the rowing becomes steadily less, rather than more, coordinated, which means that we have to work harder to maintain our speed. We end up somewhere near the bottom of the league table.

That evening we sport our blue-and-burgundy club blazers once more for posterity's sake (after all, it'll probably be the last time) and head for one of Boston's better-known bars.

'A jug of beer and five glasses,' Martin generously instructs the barman.

'What kind?'

'Dunno. Any kind will do, ta.'

We're fortunate enough to locate an empty table and five chairs, seeing that the bar is crowded. Taking delivery of our first jug, Martin orders four more – one of which goes directly into Barney's yard-of-ale glass. We warm up the ale using hands and thighs. If too cold, drinking a yard can be tough on the sinuses. A good ten minutes later, Barney is ready to go, or so we think.

'Sorry, guys, I can't let you drink that here …' The bar manager has spotted Barney's contraption and has come over.

'Huh?'

'I cannot let you drink that here.'

'And why on earth not?'

'I cannot take responsibility for you hurting yourself while doing – that,' he says, pointing at Barney, and hands us an empty jug to pour the ale into. Steadfast in his commitment to drink a yard of ale come what may, and seeing that the manager has wandered off, Barney begins to refill his glass, now hidden from view in its home-made styrofoam-and-duct-tape container. We finish our fifth and last jug and head off to an Irish pub just off Central Square, 'more sympathetic' to Barney's bravery, or so a friendly bystander tells us.

Having arrived at a colourful joint called The People's Republic, Barney lifts his yard-of-ale glass out of its silvery tube (still filled to the brim with snatched ale) and rapidly attracts attention. In no time at all we're surrounded by locals wondering who we are and what the glass is all about and whether we've ever won Henley. Barney, intoxicated by the excitement of it all, demonstrates his art by emptying the yard in one go, turning the glass ever so slightly anti-clockwise as the ale begins its journey into his gullet.

His efforts are rewarded with a round of applause. One of the locals wants a try too, using a much fizzier Bud Light, no less.

'It'll go all over the place!' Barney snorts over the noise. To our surprise, however, things go rather well, and Barney's challenger downs the stuff without spilling a drop. Barney answers with a yard of Guinness. And sure enough, he does us proud, knocking back the black nectar triumphantly and to much admiration from his public. Then he's off to the loo.

The music beats heavily on our anaesthetised minds. The pong of sweat and stale beer seems stronger now than before. The crowd too has got livelier. Then, out of nowhere, comes a curious spectator, limping his way to our table, pushing others aside. His hair is white, matted, and uncombed; his dark green coat stained and tired, his skin a translucent grey.

'I can do that ...!' the old geezer hollers in a thick Bostonian accent. 'Watch ...'

He bends down, pulls up a soiled trouser leg and yanks off what appears to be an artificial limb – a hollow stump with a black knob at the far end of it. He raises it into the air triumphantly, grabs a pint of Guinness from our table, pours it into his peg leg, and downs it in one fell swoop.

'Bloody hell …' Martin looks at him in disbelief. Then he laughs. James laughs. Mary laughs. Barney (though he won't remember any of this tomorrow) laughs. Our new American friends laugh too. The old guy laughs, beige gums exposed, saliva dribbling from a corner of his mouth. What a moment – that rare instant of pure, unadulterated joy, of freedom – a foretaste of nirvana. It's all so fucking surreal.

In the yellow cab back to our lodgings, Barney falls asleep almost immediately, legs stretched out across the back seat, his back and head leaning at an odd angle against the car door and window. His final words sum up the evening: 'Here we come, four guys in silly blazers, and these people treat us as friends …' True enough. Back at our hotel, James and I pay off the taxi driver. Barney meanwhile remains fast asleep and, had it not been for some quick thinking on our part, the driver would have made off with Barney blissfully unconscious on the back seat.

'You sure you're okay?' I ask.

'Yeah …' He smiles broadly and slowly but happily. He gives me a thumbs-up, which I take as my cue to leave. I get undressed and crawl under the static hotel blankets, glance at my alarm clock, and fart.

It's 2am.

Sunday, 22 October

Feeling a little roughed up after last night's bout of drinking, I'm finally able to catch up with the CUBC squad. Their all-important race is slated for early this afternoon. I make my way to Harvard's crimson boathouse and sit down on its wooden dock, a take-away latte in hand. I spot the crew. Duncan calls them into the boathouse for a last-minute chat. The German-made racing shell is off the racks and onto trestles for a final inspection. Footplates are checked and adjusted. Top nuts are tightened. The guys crowd around, edgy. Duncan takes a deep breath: 'You know what you've got to do, boys,' he says, and gives each of them some specific instructions. His talk is to the point. Princeton (who comprise the US national squad and are starting one place ahead of Cambridge) have got to be done away with as soon as possible. If so, there will be no further crews to pass, and we will thus have to force ourselves to row hard without other crews to pass or push off of. Not an easy thing to do by any means.

The guys nod, lift the Empacher shell to heads then shoulders, and walk it out to the dock. By now the adrenaline is surging through my body. I feel sick to my stomach.

'Wish I could do it for them,' I tell Duncan.

'No disrespect, but I really don't think that's a good idea ...'

Of course it isn't.

At Boston's Logan airport I get a text from Duncan to tell me that Cambridge came a 'disappointing eighth'. It doesn't take long for the email wash-up to surface.

From: Duncan Holland
To: Squad
Subject: HORC
Date: 23 Oct 2006 13:08:12 +0000

Gentlemen,

Circumstances mean that we haven't been able to have a full wash up yet. I will raise a few points in this mail and would like you all to contribute anything you wish to say.

Positives: The crew achieved some impressive speed. There was a general consensus about what constitutes a good rhythm. There were times when the boat was moving very well and everyone felt comfortable. We went out in the race intending to be proactive, to make things happen. We didn't achieve what we wanted but the approach was good, the first part of the race went as we wanted.

Negatives: 8th place! Failing to put Princeton away when we were

49

six seats up. This was due to a combination of factors, a bad call from Russ didn't help, and the crew lost rhythm and swing.

Things to learn / change: keep the positive, aggressive, proactive attitude. Learn how to move up, go faster, put a crew away without losing rhythm.

Comments?

Duncan

Duncan's emphasis on rhythm is telling. If only Cambridge had maintained theirs they might have put Princeton behind them quite easily. Instead, Russ called for an increase in the number of strokes per minute, inadvertently destroying whatever rhythm the crew had settled into.

From: Sebastian Schulte
To: Squad
Subject: Re: HORC
Date: 23 Oct 2006 13:29:19 +0000

I agree to all points which Duncan made, but also wanted to add the following things:

We must have more confidence in Russ's calls and actions. If he makes a mistake, we tell him afterwards, but it must not happen that the cox is corrected during the rowing permanently from the middle of the boat. It didn't happen in the performance, but it happened before and afterwards. Example. Kip made the point that the water was shallow. Fair point. Russ said that he got it, but afterwards three people in the middle of the boat kept commenting where the best line to steer was. Very annoying and not helpful at all. If Russ fucks it up by hitting the ground, it's his responsibility. Whoever eventually will be cox of the blue boat deserves full trust of the crew. Each of us rowers has enough things to work on. As Duncan said in Boston, there is no one who is that good that he can afford working on other's problems.

I think, we ought to be more critical with our performance after each outing, race etc. It's good to be positive about things, but we will win the boat race only, if we keep working hard and keep benchmarking ourselves based on high standards.

A lot of good things happened that weekend, we had a level of aggression which we never had last year. Now we need to combine this level of aggression with much more cleverness. We had this poor result only because we wanted to kill them with brute force.

See you later.

Seb

Seb, together with his close friend and German crewmate Thorsten, won gold at the 2007 World Championships in Eton. By then he had already taken home two bronze (2001 and 2005) and one silver medal (2002), as well as gold at the Under-23 World Championships. Tall and blond like Thorsten but far more assertive, Seb has just entered his third year as a PhD student. With two Boat Race losses behind him already, he is understandably critical of anything that could put his third, and probably last, attempt at risk.

His response in turn triggers a reply from Russ:

From: Russ Glenn
To: Squad
Subject: Re: Re: HORC
Date: 23 Oct 2006 14:07:03 +0000

Figured I would weigh in quickly in between cleaning up the wreckage of unpacking. I agree with the opinions thus far voiced, and agree completely with my individual criticisms as well. I'll return to that in just a second.

I think the most fundamental point to take away from this weekend is a tactical realization: if we are approaching these early season races as practice for a boat race situation, then not 'putting away' a crew when we have the opportunity is a terrible mistake. This weekend, when we were next to Princeton 5, 6, 7 seats up, there needs to be a crew wide realization that THIS is the opportunity, and the race MUST be controlled in the next couple seconds. It happens in the pattern, and with technical retention, but the attack is a commitment, with no thought to eventual sustainability. We'll make it happen by being willing to do what the crew next to us is not.

51

When I called to take the rating up and move for 15 I was trying to implement the standard 'two-man move' that Cambridge has used since I've been here the last two years. In retrospect it was a bad call – we hadn't practiced that kind of attack, and it would have been better to keep the focus more simple on the second half rhythm. However, there still needs to be a feeling of needed imminent action throughout the crew, a switch that flicks on throughout the boat that an opportunity is being presented that we must capitalize on. Such a chance may only last for a stroke or two, and we have to buy in totally. We talk about making things happen and taking risks, and now we have to implement it.

As has been said, the way in which I called that move was not what was needed. I think that was a symptom of not having practiced how we were going to do that exactly, and am absolutely confident in my and the boat's ability to respond in the correct way come April. I've gone over the tape a couple times since, and will do with Duncan as well, so that we may better address it.

When we go to the line on April 7th, I want to feel invincible. I want to have uncrackable faith that we will beyond a shadow of a doubt win. That's an achievable goal, and I look forward to moving forward to achieving it.

Putney to Mortlake, without excuses or inhibitions,

r

CHAPTER 8

Sunday, 1 October

'Let's break some hearts this morning!' Duncan looks up from his laptop. 'Never nice, but what's got to be done has got to be done. You okay staying around for the next bit?'

He looks at Grant, who nods. I'm invited to stay too to witness my first 'binning' exercise, one of many to come, no doubt, as he summons the first half-dozen boys. It's pretty heartless, frankly, but then selection invariably is, no matter that the boys walk into this eyes wide open. The rule is that anyone, at any time, is liable to be called into the Coaches' Room to be told that he's been weighed and found wanting, that he's reached the end of his useful life and has started to slow the boat down, that it's nothing personal of course but a reflection of the rest of the squad being in comparatively better shape, and that he's welcome to join the Dev squad or to try again next year.

Having been summoned to the upstairs room, they are well aware of what's about to hit them. Their body language says it all as they dribble in, resigned. The next minute is merely ritualistic. Grant stops checking his email. I put down my Moleskine pad and biro. The room is eerily quiet. Duncan swivels his chair around and faces them.

'Sorry guys, but the ride for this year is over. There's no need to take it personal, but you just aren't competitive enough compared with the rest of the squad. You've not got up to speed as quickly as them and it doesn't make sense to keep you here. Between now and April we won't be able to get you up to the level required' –

and then, as if to squash any remaining glimmer of hope – '... not even for the reserve crew.' Everyone avoids eye contact lest this causes embarrassment. Duncan continues.

'We can tell you how to improve for next year, but not now as there are too many of you and we've got training to do. Come and see us sometime next week if you want some individual pointers. But for now that's it, the end of the road. Unpleasant for you, and not particularly nice for us to have to do, but so it goes.'

The boys shuffle around awkwardly, careful not to upset the solemnity of the moment. Except for Boris. The only one genuinely shocked at being binned, he wants to know why. Duncan dismisses him, swivelling his chair back to face the paperwork on his desk. Boris, however, is not to be dissuaded.

'I didn't have more than two outings, whereas Russ and—'

'Not now, Boris,' Duncan interrupts. 'Happy to give you feedback but not today.' Agitated, he fires up his laptop and mutters something under his breath. Boris, unhappily, takes his leave and is never seen again, not for pointers, not for anything. I did, months later, catch sight of him on the River Cam, in command of his college crew in preparation for the Mays,* still looking wounded.

Though Duncan's announcement took a mere 60 seconds, in terms of impact it may have decided the future course of six careers. Unless successful some other season, they will never be part of that Cosa Nostra of rowing Blues, that closely-knit syndicate of friends united by what they put behind them on that apocalyptic day, on that sepulchral Boat Race course: vulnerability for those who won, dignity for those who didn't.

---

*The name traditionally given to the four-day 'bumps' races on the Cam in early June, in which boats are lined up one-and-a-half lengths apart with the explicit aim of 'bumping' the crew ahead and taking their place in the line-up the following day.

CHAPTER 9

I wake up to a dreary and wet outside. The weather is dispiriting, the prolonged dullness stifling. Grey skies tick by like minutes in a dentist's chair. It's raining hard enough to justify waterproofs, yet not cold enough not to work up a sweat when wearing them. Glum stuff either way.

Today's training schedule is a carbon copy of that of most other days: two consecutive 40-minute pieces on the ergs, followed by 18 kilometres on the water after lunch. As a variation on the usual tedium of erging, Russ decides he'll call the final 17 minutes of the second 40-minute piece as if it were the Boat Race, just so the boys can get used to visualising the Championship course during training. The rating throughout will remain capped at 20 strokes per minute.

Duncan nods approvingly, standing about with arms crossed over a hand-knitted brown-grey sweater, observing the athletes as they dispatch the kilometres. Russ, meanwhile, digital watch in hand, paces in between the rows of ergs, his voice picking up a pitch or two as he takes charge:

'Okay, Cambridge, you're lining up for the start—

'Oxford's beside you now—

'Ready to go—

'Umpire is ready—

'Ready Cambridge?

'GO!

'Wind for five—

'Over the next 45 seconds we're bringing it up to full racing speed—

'We're rowing past London Rowing Club—
'And you're two seats up—
'We're rowing past the black buoy now—
'We're pushing away—
'We'll be into the Fulham bend in 15 seconds—
'Swinging now into Fulham bend – and swing – swing – swing
– swing—'

The boys continue to erg as usual, still rating only 20 strokes per minute, but intensely focused on images from the Championship course projected in their minds, Russ at the controls.

'You're one seat up going into the bend—
'Swing—
'Good—
'Swing—
'Twenty seconds off the bend—
'Keep the speed up—
'Cambridge you're coming out of the Fulham bend—
'Swing – swing and contrast—
'Fulham bend to Harrods is the "kill zone"—'

What Russ refers to as the 'kill zone' is a stretch of the course, starting at about a mile or so into the race and past the first bend, where either crew will attempt a first hard push to try to get ahead of the other crew and be first into the long Surrey bend.

'I want to be three seats up by the time we reach Harrods – swing – swing—
'We're past the mile post now, Cambridge—
'Oxford is taking a mighty push—
'They're one seat up—
'Push with the legs—
'Good, Cambridge—
'Go for the push—
'Swing – swing – swing – swing—
'Move back up, Cambridge—
'There we go—
'This is your bend now—

'Into the Surrey bend—
'It's time to move—
'From Harrods to St Paul's now—
'You're going to take half a length—
'Ready?
'NOW!'

Russ is calling for a mighty push. Looking at the digital displays on their ergs, I can see that the boys have started to up the rating, wrapped up in the excitement of rowing the course, even if only in their imaginations.

'Move it – open up – and swing away—
'That's it—
'Coming into Hammersmith—
'We've got a good line—
'Go get two seats before St Paul's – swing – swing—
'Move away from Hammersmith Bridge—
'Keep the rhythm—
'Nice and relaxed—
'There you go, Cambridge—
'You've got 30 seconds of commitment and one seat to go—
'That's it—
'Good work, Cambridge—
'You've got your four seats—
'On the toes now for five strokes—
'Push – push – push – push – push—
'Moving from the toes now—
'Feel it up on the toes—
'We're moving away—
'We've got five seats on Oxford—
'Give us a push for ten strokes—
'NOW!
'Long – long – long – long – long—
'Time to attack—
'On the legs—
'Ready?

'GO!'

Again, the rating comes up slightly. 'Keep your rating down,'
Duncan warns. 'Just push with the legs.'

'Ten strokes—

'Legs away – legs – legs—

'Holding Oxford now—

'Two seats up—

'Legs – legs – legs – legs—

'Three seats up—

'Legs away—

'There we go, Tabs*—

'Past Chiswick's steps—

'I want two seats in the bend—

'Thirty seconds – two seats—

'Thirty seconds—

'NOW!

'Swing – swing – swing – swing – swing—

'Moving one seat—

'That's it, Tabs—

'We're four seats up on Oxford—

'This is the Oxford bend—

'We're four seats up—

'You know they're going to come at you—

'Here you go, Cambridge—

'We're gonna kill their dreams—

'You give them no seats—

'Bow side, hold your finishes—

'Bold sweeps – bold sweeps—

'Oxford has taken one seat—

'We're taking two back under the bridge—

*Oxford have for many years referred to their Cambridge rivals with the slang term
'Tabs'. Cambridge does not, as far as I know, have a slang equivalent for Oxford
(though, thanks to Seb's creativity, we have begun to refer to them as 'Scump'; being
German, Seb hadn't realised that 'scum' is spelled without a 'p' at the end, and the
word stuck).

'NOW!
'Move away—
'On the legs—
'Two minutes to go now, Cambridge—
'Four seats up—
'Oxford is tired—
'They've got nothing left—
'Last few seconds—
'We're gonna break 'em—
'Take it up—
'One big acceleration—
'Five big strokes—
'GO!
'Accelerate – accelerate—
'Now move it!
'Five seats up—
'Get me six—
'That's it, Tabs—
'Six seats—
'Twenty-five seconds—
'We're going ten strokes—
'On the swing—
'NOW!
'Swing – swing – swing – swing – swing—
'Ten seconds – swing away – swing—
'Two more, Tabs—
'Moving away—
'See you later, assholes ...'

At that the boys stop rowing. My heart and head are pounding as I try to keep up with Russ's calls, my biro sprinting across the pages of my pad, blood rushing through my veins. So too is the adrenaline, for in seventeen short minutes the atmosphere in The Goldie lies transformed – looks of boredom having given way to exhilaration and anticipation – the exercise intended to help the squad visualise the Boat Race course, leaving no surprises for race day but, instead, reproducing all the familiar landmarks at about the right time into the race.

Visualisation has become a popular tool in enhancing performance in sports generally, not just in rowing. We do surprisingly little of it in Cambridge, or less than I expected anyway, given pretty persuasive evidence of its beneficial effects. Especially in top sports where tiny margins separate gold from silver and bronze, any extra bit of performance helps. And it's here that visualisation can help rowers raise their game to the next level.

Like Russ's attempt this morning, visualisation requires oarsmen to create a mental image of what they want to happen and feel during a race, images that can be visual, sensory or auditory. Their effectiveness is directly contingent on the level of detail that can be imagined – the more detailed the image, the more effective the exercise. Summoning the powers of imagination, oarsmen can call up these images over and over, enhancing skill through sheer repetition, similar to what they would ordinarily do in physical practice. And after a while, their bodies become trained to perform the skill imagined – precisely as it was imagined.

At a different level, visualisation can help rowers cope with pre-race anxiety by forcing them to imagine themselves repeating their best-ever performance, but in the context of the current race. It may help them get used to the idea of winning, to not freeze in the headlights when realising that they're ahead and closing in on the finish line and that this perhaps shouldn't be, that a win wouldn't be deserved, that one oughtn't to be moving ahead. Visualisation helps one get used to winning, knowing that one is allowed to win – that it's okay to be better at something than anyone else.

CHAPTER 10

The excitement of the morning digested, we pack into two white vans en route to our other boathouse in Ely. The lunch we miss out on before the ride we scoff down during it: hot fare scooped out of Tupperwares, peanut-butter-and-jam sandwiches whipped up en route, flapjacks, malt loaves, hot cross buns, and the odd boiled egg – the bowels of the van a curious melange of sulphur, cabbage, peanuts and boiled rice. Seb fiddles obsessively with the air vents.

In contrast to recent years, water training has come to include increasing amounts of side-by-side racing, where two crews (in eights or fours) row alongside each other at full pressure but at a capped rating (meaning that both crews are limited to a fixed number of strokes per minute, usually somewhere between 20 and 28). This helps fuel competition within the squad and mimics racing conditions. After all, the Boat Race is rowed side-by-side from Putney to Mortlake, or at least until one of the crews gets sufficiently far ahead to take 'the best line' to the finish line. At a more subtle level, this particular exercise forces rowers to keep their eyes in their own boats and not give in to the temptation to steal a look at how well their crew is doing with respect to the one racing alongside. 'Keep your eyes in your own damn boat!' is a familiar call, suggesting that any lapse of concentration or any unnecessary body movement (even the sideways movement of the head) may bring the boat off-balance and destroy its rhythm. Boat speed is, in large measure, a function of rhythm, and this is only ever achieved through synchronisation of effort, a perfect coordination between coxswain and oarsman, boat and oarsman, oarsman and oarsman. As Robin Williams, CUBC's former coach, explains:

> Rowing is a strange sport – it's like a puzzle. There are other sports where you work as a team, but you can't have fifteen guys holding the ball at the same time. In a rowing boat you've got to work to capacity individually, but have some sort of feeling for the whole crew to apply that power in unison. It's a massive discipline. If one person falters then it breaks the chain and the whole thing collapses pretty instantaneously.[13]

It's easy to see why the River Great Ouse makes for better training than Cambridge's own River Cam. Aside from the occasional holiday cruiser, fisherman's launch or sculler, the river offers a near-empty stretch of water including a perfectly straight 5-kilometre reach, ideal for side-by-side paddling. The weather today is about as inhospitable as it can be, with freezing rain which chills to the bone, and with nothing but a church steeple to stop Ural mountain winds from howling across the Fens. And it's here, in this explosive stretch, that Cambridge's competitive spirit is contrived and then honed. And then honed some more. I empathise with the oarsmen and coxswains who have little or no protection from the elements except what body heat they can themselves generate. I zip up my fleece, my gilet and waterproofs, and pull a woollen hat over my eyes.

Duncan stands up in a second coaching launch – bobbing up and down like ours does on the grumpy Ouse – his movements restricted by his bright all-weather gear. Protruding from his hood is a megaphone, the only living link between us and them, between 'we who see' and 'they who feel' what the rowing is like. With a wind-garbled '*Cambridge. Attention. Go!*', the boats spring off the starting line and into the 5-kilometre stretch, zigzagging through the liquid chocolate. One of them is unable to keep a straight line and veers into the riverbank. Ordered to cross over to the left, and more exposed, side of the river to create more space for the other, it does so without enthusiasm, the crew ending up too close to the riverbank and causing Dan to catch the reeds with his oar. His blade-handle slaps painfully into his gut. Getting your oar caught in weeds or the water is a deeply unpleasant experience. It invariably happens when one least expects it, surrendering oar and oarsman to the forces of nature, often brutally slicing across the victim who is forced flat on his back. Needless to say, Dan is livid as he scrambles to recover his position, his immediate response a colourful string of expletives directed at the coxswain.

Then, with 300 metres to go, their coxswain calls for a final surge. The boat responds immediately and, at last, begins to pick up some respectable speed. Colin Scott, veteran of two Goldie races and winner of the Ladies' Challenge Plate at Henley Royal Regatta, becomes incensed now too, at this sudden surge after what felt like a needlessly heavy row.

'What the fuck was that all about?!' he shouts across the howling wind just as soon as their coxswain calls for the crew to 'easy all' (the command to stop rowing). Why did the boat suddenly pick up when asked for a push, when feeling bloody heavy and slow through most of the 5-kilometre stretch, seeing that there was plenty of energy left in the crew? 'You just cannot do that!' He turns to face those sitting behind him in the boat. 'You've got to give it all in a race. It doesn't matter if you're behind or ahead … There is no excuse *ever* not to give it all.'

It's the first time I have seen tempers flare up in a Cambridge boat: first Dan at their coxswain, then Colin at everyone. I expect I'll see quite a lot more of this.

CHAPTER 11

Sunday, 12 November

'Someone's brought some farties along,' Dan's sing-song voice hails from the back of the van.

'Is that you, Stutt?'

'Nope.'

'Me neither,' Marco volunteers.

'Russ?'

'Fuck no—'

'Hopper?'

A second-year History student at Peterhouse, Cambridge's oldest college, Hopper sits knees up, wedged in between two rows of seats.

'Hopper, that's fucking disgusting!'

Fear has a smell, as love does, mused Margaret Atwood. The guys this morning are nervous, as is Duncan, keen to get the day's duties over and done with. Today is important selection-wise, and the first time the boys will perform in full view of the media. We're heading for Birmingham's National Indoor Arena to compete in the British Indoor Rowing Championship – an event that, over the years, has become an integral part of selection for the Oxford and Cambridge crews. Unusually, however, Oxford has decided to part with tradition and stay put. We take turns speculating why such might be the case. Is it because they don't want us to know what they're capable of? Is it because this year they lack the equivalents of our Thorsten Engelmann and Kieran West? Are they hoping to have a peek at our hand of cards but without us seeing theirs too?

The Birmingham arena itself is depressing in its functionality. We congregate in upstairs Block 5: an eerily vacant cluster of bright red canvas seats bolted to vast concrete slabs, the whole shebang brightly lit by fluorescent tubes. Posters advertising the wares of corporate sponsors hang off the unpainted grey, inviting us to partake of the sickly sweet energy drinks on offer.

Some 30 feet below us, 140 Concept II ergs stand proudly, neatly lined up in rows of twenty like Emperor Qin's terracotta army. In due course, they'll be mounted by different generations of rowers – 3,000 in all – competing for the fastest time over a virtual 2,000-metre course in the biggest championship of its kind anywhere in the world.

The squad, meanwhile, sit quietly, pensively, fiddling with their bags, reading the odd paperback, or, in most cases, snatching the odd free half-hour to catch up with their academic work. This has always been a challenge: to succeed not just in sports but academically. And so a heavy premium is set on time – unless they are on the ergs, lifting weights, stretching or rowing, they are invariably found buried in books and papers, frantically preparing the next morning's essay.

Kieran and Thorsten avoid each other. They even travelled up in separate vans. It's not that they don't like each other – it's just that they are so close in strength. They know the world will be watching as they battle it out, side-by-side, in two hours from now. Today will be the first public display of a subtle but profound and long-standing rivalry between them. Kieran, no doubt, is keen to better last year's narrow defeat by his German rival Thorsten. Having led for most of the way, he was passed by Thorsten in the final few metres and beaten to the punch by a mere 0.1 seconds (the smallest measurable margin). Kieran will want to make good today and defend his turf as the only Olympic medallist in the squad. A three-time Cambridge Blue, he won gold in the Men's Eight in the 2000 Sydney Olympics and subsequently a World Championship gold medal.

Standing a towering 6ft 8in, Kieran began his rowing career as a coxswain aged ten for Kingston Rowing Club, soon growing too tall and taking up sculling instead (rowing in a single with two oars, one in each hand, much like a traditional rowing boat but much thinner and lighter). There were very few scullers as young as him, and so he ended up spending much of his early rowing career navigating the Thames in solitude. His age would have made him ideally suited to sculling; youngsters can learn how to balance a single comparatively quickly. Besides, sculling is symmetrical, whereas sweep rowing is not, and thus much less hard on the backs of growing oarsmen. Even so, Kieran sustained a nasty back injury when training for the GB squad in 1994, aged only sixteen, which forced him out of rowing and into physiotherapy.

He returned to rowing three years later as an undergraduate at Christ's College. After all, he'd liked it, been bloody good at it as a kid, was miles ahead of everyone else on the erg, had won medals, liked winning, and loved competing.

Having rowed for Christ's in the Mays, Kieran trialled with CUBC in September 1997. He had begun sweep-rowing only that year (having sculled until his arrival at Christ's), but based on his erg scores and GB trial results earned himself a place in Goldie (the reserve crew). That year, Goldie was unusually problematic, even if potentially very fast. Its stern four had failed to make the Blue Boat and had found it difficult to reconcile themselves to competing as reserves instead. Its bow four had never expected to make the Blue Boat in any case and were content to have made it as far as Goldie. Tension between the stern four and bow four erupted just before the Boat Race, and suffice it to say that they never lived up to their potential. Ever since, Kieran always remained sensitive to tensions between, and within, the two Cambridge crews. Moreover, losing his first race for Cambridge was an experience more gutting than anything he had been through before, and one he promised himself never to repeat. He upped his performance the following season and made the winning Blue Boat in 1999 and again, as President, in 2001. His GB debut saw him take home silver at the 1999 World Championship Men's Eight, followed by gold in 2002, silver in 2003, a fourth place in 2005, fifth place in 2006, and an MBE for services to rowing in the 2001 New Year's Honours List. He's the oldest triallist at 29 and the only member of the current squad to have previously won the Boat Race.

The German international, Thorsten Engelmann, is four years his junior. Like Kieran, he took up rowing at a young age. As a nine-year-old he would join his father at his rowing club, and soon developed a taste for rowing himself. He went on to win bronze twice at the World Championships (2001 and 2005), silver (2002), gold at the Under-23 World Championships in 2000, the Henley Grand in 2005, and World gold in 2006. Though Thorsten doesn't know it yet, he will make history this year as the heaviest-ever oarsman to compete in the Boat Race, weighing in at an impressive 17st 6lb 4oz (110.8kg). There's a reason for this too, as we will soon see.

Their rivalry today is fuelled by hopes of stroking the Blue Boat. After all, it's up to stroke to set the rhythm and to communicate with the coxswain during the race. He's also the public face of the crew, the one oarsman in full view of the cameras. As for Kieran, he saw himself as Kip's natural successor, having done a good job stroking the British Eight in the 2005 World Championships and 2006 World Cup, and having stroked the 2002 Coxed Four to a gold medal. Gutted at having lost last year's race, each will have been keen to try to settle into a strong rhythm from the start. The question of who will ultimately make the better stroke lingers uncomfortably in the air. It's too early in the season to tell. Even so, whatever the outcome, selecting a stroke from two foolhardy individuals, each of whom thinks himself best suited for the job, will invariably generate a fair amount of heat. No one's broached the topic, even though everyone is fully cognizant of it. Kip McDaniel, having formerly stroked several successful Harvard crews, yet a losing Blue Boat too, is unlikely to join the contest. Last April's five-length defeat still weighs heavily on his shoulders.

And despite Kip possessing the aggression and consistency of rhythm required, this trauma wants a fresh start on a clean slate with a new face in stroke seat. Psychology trumps physiology – and not for the first, nor last, time this season.

With two hours to go, Duncan stands up to face the squad and make his pitch. This is, he says, CUBC's first event in England, and as much part of the Boat Race campaign as anything else. 'You're here to lay down a marker for yourselves and for Oxford. Oxford should be here but are afraid of showing their cards, and so we want to make sure that when they see our scores, they go, "Oooh shit—".' As usual, his talk is short and to the point. We're here to put down numbers. It is as simple as that.

That said, he wanders off to treat the coaching staff to coffee. Some of the guys disperse to have a look around the arena. Others grab a book or laptop and resume their work, legs stretched out defiantly across the seat in front. And so they wait, and I with them.

With 30 minutes to go, I make my way down to the holding area where the squad are warming up. Unsurprisingly, the guys are introspective and avoid eye contact or even the most casual of conversations. This is their time to find focus, to get their every square inch, every nerve and fibre, alert for the approaching battle. Even if I'm not participating, I can feel the adrenaline sprint through my system. I'm actually nervous.

With five minutes remaining, the athletes mount their Concept II workhorses, Thorsten in pole position with Kieran immediately to his left and Seb to his right. At the starting signal, Thorsten and Kieran assume a commanding lead and remain tantalisingly close for the first four minutes of the race. Even up to the last 500 metres, it's far from obvious which of the two will take home the gold. Then, with only 250 metres to go, Thorsten boldly raises the stakes by driving his splits down to 1:24. Kieran is unable to match this sprint to the finishing line and ends a close second. Thorsten wins in 5:52.3; Kieran comes in at 5:54.6; Seb is third in 5:56.7. Compared to Siejkowski's world record of 5:37.0 and the

British record of 5:42.3 set by Pinsent, these are very respectable performances. They are the only three to have come in at under six minutes in their event, taking gold, silver and bronze respectively. As they wander off to get changed, Thorsten grabs Kieran from behind in a great big bear hug, as if to bury the day's hatchet. Kieran smirks in reply, grateful for the gesture, too tired to do much else.

In the changing area I find most of the boys stretching or warming down on one of the ergs. Wanne, who equalled his personal best (PB) at 6:13.5, is in a bad state.

'It's always like this,' he mumbles. 'I always feel miserable afterwards, like a dog, that's the terrible part.'

And, frankly, he looks it. So too does Patrick, whom I discover behind a curtained-off area, out of the public eye, sitting with his back against a wall, next to a foam-crested puddle of sick.

'Cheers,' he says, as I hand him a wad of paper towels.

'Whatever happened here?'

'I dunno – I just felt terribly nauseous.'

(Long pause as he collects his breath and I my thoughts.)

'You know, the funny thing is that I forgot to set my machine to display my splits. All the time I had no way of knowing how fast I was going, all I could see was the distance rowed, and if only I had known my splits, I wouldn't have gone off as fast as I did, but kept something in store for the end, and I might have broken 6:20. Shite –'

He breathes heavily and with difficulty, his body glistening with perspiration, his short, matted locks glued to his forehead. A janitor arrives on the scene, mop and soapy bucket in tow.

'Sorry about that.'

'No worries, mate.'

❖

Duncan sends the crew an email that evening.

From: Duncan Holland
To: Squad
Subject: BIRC
Date: 12 Nov 2006 18:33

Team,

Attached are the results from today's race.

12 PB's from 21 starters is excellent, a true sign that you are working well, and that the training programme is working.

The results are very similar to those from last year, detailed analysis will follow.

Well done to all those who posted a PB.

For those who were disappointed, take the time on Tuesday to talk to me or one of the other coaches, but also remember that this is but one test. Our next challenge is the Fours Head next week, and there we will be racing OUBC, not ourselves!

P to M*

Back at The Goldie, the coaches sit down for a meeting of minds. The squad's performance at the Indoors has left everyone fairly happy, with the exception of Rebecca. She worries the coaches.

'She's lovely, don't get me wrong,' says Duncan, 'and technically quite good, but I worry that she might crack under pressure – I mean look at what happened today when she didn't do a personal best on the ergs.' He forces his chair back, his feet resting on his desk. Rebecca, having joined the boys for their 2,000-metre attempt but faring worse, had been so upset by her performance that she had broken down in tears.

Tom moves forward in his seat. Though a common enough sight at the CUBC, involving athletes in selection is highly unusual. In most clubs, coaches have absolute control over selection. In Cambridge, however, coaches advise the President on

---

* 'P to M' is the traditional way of signing off email correspondence within CUBC. It stands for 'Putney to Mortlake', this being the Boat Race or Championship course.

selection, and he, ordinarily, will follow their guidance. Tom says what seems to be on everyone's mind:

'The worst thing that could happen is that she'd crack up during the warm-up to the Boat Race.'

'True,' nods Duncan, 'and that is a risk we cannot afford to take. No way.'

That night I sleep badly, marred by dreams of failure, and wake up conscious of my rapidly beating heart. The room feels stuffy and warm, the duvet heavy and damp. Roxana must have closed the window last night before getting into bed. It's too early to wake up and yet too late to ease back into sleep. I take deep breaths, trying but failing to keep my demons at bay. I suspect that if there's anything shared between oarsman and ethnographer it's a struggle for survival: a shared sense of oppression, of being forced into a corner by the manifold demands of being a student of both books and the body.

CHAPTER 12

Friday, 17 November

I seem to be in a playhouse but it's not one I recognise. It's a theatre all right, even if it has none of the usual tell-tale signs: no velvety chairs (no chairs at all as far as I can make out), no heavy curtains and no chandeliers, and the stage looks fatigued, its floorboards stained with the residue of once popular but long since forgotten pantomimes. On the stage, and around me, are children, two dozen in all, but too short for their age and too tetragonal too, like characters out of a mean Japanese comic. They smile at me incessantly without a care in the world save to please me, all but their faces obscured by banded fluorescent costumes, so that with the lights dimmed all one sees are blue, green, yellow and orange lines dancing around in black space.

I appear to have been cast as a lion but have difficulty putting on a credible performance and can't seem to make up my mind whether to stand on my hind legs or make do on hands and knees, and I don't now recollect how the matter was decided in the end, but I do recall a faint hum as if from a distant world, annoying and yet strangely familiar. I have no idea why I'm here, or why I was cast as a lion, or who these little people are and what my relationship is to them …

I wake up to a much less colourful world. Gone are the dancing fluorescent stripes and little people, their festivities, smiles and costume. I reach sideways to press the snooze button. Last night's half bottle of red has extracted its pound of flesh and 'made such a torch of the beast's breath that the spectators had difficulty in holding their ground against it'.[14] I feel parched, pooped, confused – haunted by the ghosts of last night's dreams. Why have they become so vivid, so menacing, so wounding? Who are these vengeful shadows from the netherworld floating in and out of my head, and why are they here? Am I not allowed some reprieve from the excessive introspection and worry that have enveloped me like candyfloss since joining the squad? Like Larkin's mum and dad, the boys fuck you up: 'They may not mean to but they do/They fill you with faults they had/And add some extra, just for you.'[15]

I shuffle my way onto the plastic bathroom floor, drop my boxers, and study myself in the bathroom mirror. Having seen how well-hung the squad are, I've become fixated on my own member. I look down past my stomach, turning now sideways and then facing forwards, varying the angle, the object the same, the point the same. I examine its reflection in the cracked mirror, mount the tub, turn the taps, and draw the curtain.

Wikipedia: Main article:

Human penis size

As a general rule, an animal's penis is proportional to its body size, but this varies greatly between species – even between closely related species. For example, an adult gorilla's erect penis is about 4cm (1.5in) in length; an adult chimpanzee, significantly smaller (in body size) than a gorilla, has a penis size about double that of the gorilla. In comparison, the human penis is larger than that of any other primate, both in proportion to body size and in absolute terms.

While results vary across studies, the consensus is that the average human penis is approximately 12.7–15cm (5–5.9in) in length and 12.3cm (4.85in) in circumference when fully erect. The average penis size is slightly larger than the median size. Most of these studies were performed on subjects of primarily European descent; worldwide averages may vary.

A research project, summarizing dozens of published studies conducted by physicians of different nationalities, shows that worldwide, erect-penis size averages vary between 9.6cm (3.7in) and 16cm (6.2in). It has been suggested that this difference is caused not only by genetics, but also by environmental factors such as culture, diet, chemical/pollution exposure, etc.

As with any other bodily attribute, the length and girth of the penis can be highly variable between individuals of the same species. In many animals, especially mammals, the size of a flaccid penis is much smaller than its erect size. In humans and some other species, flaccid vs. erect penis size varies greatly between individuals, such that penis size when flaccid is not a reliable predictor of size when erect.

Except for extreme cases at either end of the size spectrum, penis size does not correspond strongly to reproductive ability in almost any species.

Useful that.*

Immediately following an urgent email from The Desk of Mr Pascal Kabore, Eco Bank, Burkina Faso, is a message from Duncan

---

*An amusing essay, written by a woman, on the matter of penis size is Susan Bordo's 'Does Size Matter?' In it, she reveals details that I suspect most men don't know about (I didn't). For example, did you know that the warlords of the Ottoman Empire publicly posted their genital measurements for conquering tribes to admire? Or that groups ranging from the Caramoja tribe of northern Uganda to the sadhus of India have long tied weights to the penis in order to make it longer (the latter apparently in the belief that God dwells in the penis), stretching it to as much as eighteen inches? Or that Jack Johnson, the first African American world heavyweight boxing champion, wrapped his penis in gauze to emphasise its size as he paraded around the ring? Or even that a female executive at Mattel Toys, in 1961, caused an uproar when suggesting that Ken, Barbie's counterpart, should have a 'bulge' in his groin (which led Mattel to experiment with three different sizes, of which embarrassed male executives had to choose one). This 'locker room' phenomenon is well documented and similar to a perception among women who think themselves 'too fat', even as their actual measurements are average. The conclusion for both sexes is, apparently, the same. Size matters, but only to the extent that it's as much a function of one's imagination as one's actual physiology. Men underestimate their proportions in very much the same way women overestimate theirs. Or so Bordo concludes. (Her essay can be found in *Revealing Male Bodies*, edited by N. Tuana, W. Cowling, M. Hamington, G. Johnson and T. MacMullan, Indiana University Press, 2002, pp. 19–37. Much of the above is quoted from her essay.)

to four members of the squad. As has become the tradition at this time of year, the squad's been divided up into groups of four for the purpose of racing the Head of the River Fours this weekend. A prominent feature on the training calendar, like its bigger brother, the race trials the Boat Race course in reverse order. One of the Fours has so far failed to impress in training. Individually they might be fine rowers, but taken together they are unable to make a go of it and spend much of their time quarrelling instead. With the Head Race only days away now, the prospect of a decent showing isn't great. Should they not rapidly improve, their own prospects within the club aren't magnificent either. After all, every trial counts, however insignificant in the larger scheme of things.

From: Duncan Holland
To: Marco Espin, Dan O'Shaughnessy, Wanne Kromdijk, Matthew Altman
Subject: Four
Date: 16 Nov 2006 19:04:52 -0000

Gentlemen!

I am disturbed by some of the reports coming out of your four. We need to address the problems, and sooner rather than later.

I want you all to be at Goldie tomorrow at 09:00 to talk about how we can make your four go better on Saturday.

Duncan

In an unusual twist of events, Duncan has asked that I mediate this discussion. It appears he has rather more confidence in my ability to defuse conflict than I have. Anxious at the prospect of facing up to four angry men, I spent much of last night reading my tattered notes on mediation and conflict resolution, acutely aware that this may well turn out to be my very own litmus test – a cerebral equivalent of the dreaded 5,000-metre erg – and that, should things go lopsided, I could be binned with the dysfunctional four. Visions of my research being flushed down the drain are too much for me to bear – and so back to my classroom notes I go.

❖

The spirits this morning have well and truly reached rock bottom. Inside the stately Captains' Room, the stale breath of 152 past crews can be felt wheezing down our necks – their painted names poignant reminders of what's at stake. The fact that the guys are willing to have this conversation at all is a good indication of how bad things have become. Ordinarily, stuff like this is sorted out either on the water or immediately afterwards. 'It's not a bloody book group,' as Bakes put it.

We grab a chair each around the large oak table. Duncan and I sit at opposite ends. Grant sits to Duncan's right. Matt next to Grant. An exceptionally bright American, Matt is in Cambridge for one year before resuming his training at Harvard Medical School. Like Jake, he learned to row at Stanford. Unlike Jake, his body doesn't resemble that of the typical oarsman: his barrel-chested torso too short for his long legs. His dark and deep-set eyes match the colour of his hair; his long fingers are folded in a gesture of sobriety.

Next to Matt, and immediately to my left, sits Marco. An Engineering undergraduate like Tom James, Marco is lighter and shorter even than Kip. The son of a Spanish immigrant who made good by building a successful London-based property empire, he learned to row at St Paul's School before coming up to Cambridge. He is one of the youngest in an environment dominated by postgraduates four or more years his senior. As he also weighs significantly less than anyone else in the squad (aside from the coxswains), he has to work doubly hard to match the power of the heavyweights. With the same fat percentage as Thorsten, Seb, Pete and Tom, Marco effectively has less muscle on his slender frame. What he has, however, he tends to use very effectively.

On the other side of Duncan sit Dan and Wanne, Dan with his elbows on the table, hands folded on his chest, his two-day stubble and broad shoulders betraying that unmistakable alpha male presence. His facial features are well defined and proportionate, with a strong jaw and clear blue eyes, and the toughness of an ice-hockey player whose coach once told him to strike first whenever he felt at risk of being attacked: 'If you think someone's going to do something to you, you do it to them first.' Aggression was to become one of Dan's trademark qualities.

The soft-spoken Wanne sits back in his chair, a stark contrast to Dan, hands folded in his lap. He's found it difficult to combine the first year of his PhD in Plant Biology with rowing, the latter being far more tiring than he anticipated. Though he rowed for years at university in Wageningen, Holland, he's never felt more exhausted.

'You all want to race on Saturday?' Duncan asks somewhat rhetorically. The table's flat surface seems to have become a de facto focal point. Duncan, hands clasped around a mug of coffee, continues:

'In that case we've got some problems to sort out, something we can only do when we're prepared to be completely honest with each other ...'

'You sure you're ready for that?' They nod. 'Right then: Marco, you steer well when you put your mind to it but are all over the bloody place when you don't, so you've got to keep up your concentration.'

'Matt, you've told me in confidence that you're unhappy with one of the team members, I won't say who.' This, of course, now places poor Matt in an awkward position, with his three crewmates looking at him curiously, wondering who this mystery member may be. His own gaze meanwhile remains firmly focused on one of the cardboard coasters on the table.

I'm growing increasingly uncomfortable.

'Dan, you were in some fast Canadian crews but we have yet to see you move a boat fast ...'

'... and Wanne, you've shown some good improvement but I know that you're unhappy, blowing your head off about the crew at home after training.'

Having thus lit the fire, Duncan leaves me to put it out, closing the door behind him. The room falls eerily silent. 'Right,' I think, 'let's do it.' Dan, Wanne, Matt and Marco spend the next three-quarters of an hour getting stuff off their chests, at long last able to offload their pent-up frustrations, knowing that for once they're being listened to – not just by Grant and me but by each other. The resulting deluge is pretty much as bad as it gets. Then, just as everyone's feeling raw and exposed, the worst possible thing happens: others come knocking on the locked door, reminding us that we're meant to be heading for Putney, and could we please wrap up and continue our conversation in London?

Agitated, we grab our stuff and leave the room – all of us, that is, except Dan. Duncan finds him lingering in the Captains' Room.

'You comin'?'

Dan looks up at Duncan. 'Nope.' And after a brief pause, 'I'm not gonna race this weekend.'

'Think about what you're doing, Dan,' Duncan responds. 'If you walk out of here and won't race this weekend, you're out of the squad!'

Dan's reply is unequivocal. He marches out of the room, down the wooden stairs, and into the downstairs changing room to collect his jacket and bag. It's there that I run into him.

'What's up?' I ask, blissfully unaware of the confrontation upstairs.

'I'm going – I'm fucking tired of this shit.'

'I told Dan that if he's walking out of here, he's walking out of CUBC,' Duncan calls from the bottom of the stairs.

This is not what I had in mind. My eyes dart to find Duncan's, and both of us look on as Dan leaves the building. Duncan is visibly upset. So am I. Having finally had a chance to prove myself to Duncan, I've well and truly blown it. Our talk was meant to bring the crew together, to allow them to get their emotions off their chest in a safe environment and, that over with, to focus on solving whatever technical problems remain. Instead it has destroyed whatever scrap of hope there might have been of reuniting the four. To think that, minutes ago, I'd been encouraged by their frank and open discussion, thinking we were on our way to a fix, at least for tomorrow's race. Now we no longer even have a crew.

Duncan and I follow the vans on their way to Putney in a rusty Citroën: 'Got it for four hundred quid from a lady owner, that's why it's done so few miles, you see?' The car meanwhile is heavy with the stale pong of cigarette smoke (though it's not inconceivable that she was a heavy smoker), and I'm well and truly off-colour by the time we reach London. Then, with only another fifteen minutes to go until we reach Putney, Duncan receives a text message.

'Can you read it to me? I'm driving.'

'Not sure who it's from, but it says: "I had a long talk with Tom and David Barst. Tom is driving me to London. I'll be there at 3pm." Think it's Dan?'

'Sounds like Dan!' Duncan squeezes his steering wheel ever so slightly. Dan appears to be on his way. The clouds may have just begun to lift, not least within the narrow confines of Duncan's Citroën.

Once Dan's arrived, the foursome and I find a quiet corner at the King's College School (KCS) boathouse to continue this morning's discussion. We improvise into a circle facing each other.

'Before we continue where we left off, anyone any comments?' I begin.

Dan coughs. I look up. So do Marco, Wanne and Matt.

'I fucked up this morning ...' His voice is raw but subdued. He tells us of his brother's suicide three years ago, after a long struggle with depression, and of how a family friend had recently lost a child too, and of how that affected his parents, bringing their own loss back into focus, and how he's now had to cope not just with a dysfunctional crew but also with his parents leaning heavily on him for moral support, and how that's draining him of every bit of energy and making him 'crazy-brain', as he puts it.

'Holy shit.'

'Yup.'

'Fuck ...'

(Expectant silence.)

'Cool,' I say, lost for anything more sensitive or appropriate. Of course what I meant to say was that Dan's cardinal admission, raw though it was, may be just what was needed to clear the air and might breathe new life into our arrested four. *Tout comprendre c'est tout pardonner.* Suddenly everyone is prepared to do his bit to make the boat go faster. The blame game of this morning is finally giving way to one focused on contributions – contributions to the solution as well as the original problem. Not ten minutes later, we are heading for the Tideway's edge, ready to put our minds to rest and our oars to use.

Saturday, 18 November

The fewer oars that there are at work on each side of a boat, the less there is to maintain the balance, meaning that a more finished style of oarsmanship is required in a four. Strength and weight, which in the centre seats of an eight may be most useful, lose their value in the four unless allied to perfect style.[16]

With 50 minutes to go until boating, and another 60 until the start of the Head of the River Fours, I find the boys assembled in their foursomes. As with nearly all races, a vast amount of time beforehand is spent waiting, watching the minutes tick by, too early for a warm-up, trying to focus the mind on the race ahead. Any race will have been won a hundred times in every serious oarsman's mind before a single starting shot has been fired, mastering the liquid course over and over but each time with slight variations: in wind and water conditions, with crews coming up from behind or having to pass a slower crew ahead, catching crabs and recovering from them. Other university squads have joined us at KCS too, sharing the boathouse but keeping very much to themselves.

When nature calls I join an already sizeable queue of heavy-weights anxious for one of only two toilet cubicles to free up. To make matters worse, only one seems to be working properly.

'Thing don't flush?' the next in the queue asks a rower as he surfaces from the left cubicle unaccompanied by the usual flushing noises.

The rower (embarrassed): 'No ...'

Next-in-the-queue: 'And you just pooped in there?'

The rower (defensive): 'What else am I supposed to do?'

Next-in-the-queue: 'You poop where you can flush, not where you can't flush.'

Thorsten and Jake, queuing slightly ahead, shrug their shoulders. What's his problem?

The Fuller's Head of the River Fours delivers some nice results for us, particularly for our combination of Thorsten, Seb, Kieran and Tom, as the 'big four', with Russ in the coxswain's seat. They were the quickest of the coxed and coxless fours on the river, quicker even than Leander's heavily-stacked crew that included Steve Williams, Alex Partridge and Peter Reed, three members of the World Championship gold-medallist coxless four. Not a bad achievement, particularly for Thorsten. As he tells me later that evening over lager and chips in the Duke's Head (a nearby pub popular with oarsmen), aside from winning their category in the Head race, what really did it for him was to have proved to Kieran, the coaches, and the squad that he would make a good stroke; that the Blue Boat would be in safe hands with him in pole position. It was this that for him constituted today's biggest achievement.

He tells me how very unpromising he was as a young oarsman and how he had often felt like throwing in the towel. After all, the more senior rowers in his German squad dismissed him as too weak and too incompetent technically to make a good oarsman. Odd, isn't it, for someone who can now pull a 5,000-metre erg at a time close to the world record, and who is a rowing World Champion? And yet despite repeated put-downs, Thorsten persisted. It may well be this ability – or if not an ability maybe it's just doggedness or simply delusions of grandeur – to pick oneself up regardless of what anyone else might say, possibly with good reason, and have another go that distinguishes the extraordinary from the merely ordinary.

When comparing the day's results for Cambridge and Oxford

(who race under the name Isis), one problem immediately becomes obvious. Even if one of our crews won its category, the spread between our crews and those of Oxford is potentially significant. Our two coxed fours finished a good 50 seconds apart, compared with a difference of only 6 seconds for Oxford's. We may well have the fastest four in the country, but the Boat Race is rowed in eights, and each eight will only ever be as fast as its weakest link. So one of our more significant challenges will be that of generating one very fast eight from oarsmen who would seem to be in different leagues when it comes to skill, strength and racing experience.

Chapter 13

Sunday, 19 November

Slept well and woke up feeling refreshed. Marco offered to host a few of us at his parents' house in Barnes Village, one of London's more affluent neighbourhoods. The house itself, a detached Victorian mansion built in the 1860s, was painstakingly renovated by his parents twenty years ago, and now houses a swimming pool (with an artificial current so strong that even with the best effort one has difficulty reaching the opposite side of the pool), a sauna, a pool room, five or six bedrooms over four floors, several reception rooms, three dogs, an in-house cinema, a kitchen with cutlery drawers three times the size of an ordinary drawer, a palm tree in front, and a big back garden complete with coach house and self-contained apartment. In all, a splendid alternative to your average accommodation.

The bright sun and morning air are wonderfully refreshing. The cold air fashions little puffs of smoke out of our warm breath as we walk briskly from Barnes Village to Putney. I rather fancy us looking like a chain of linked steam engines, smoke puffing from each in a regular rhythm, deceptively so because the pace set by Marco is debilitating. We arrive at the KCS boathouse a few minutes early.

Duncan calls the squad together for a couple of announcements. Our 'big four', he says, beat every single sweep boat on the river, including Leander's previously undefeated World Champions, so well done to them. They deserve to look smug this morn-

83

ing. Duncan then compliments the 'troubled four' on having been able to pull things together on the day after weeks of infighting and dismal rowing. The difference, he says, was psychological rather than physiological. In the last three days the crew didn't suddenly learn to row better. They simply learned to deal with the frustration of being unable to get any messages through to each other, and to apply every ounce of mental energy on race day. Their rowing on the head course was markedly faster and in every way superior to that in any previous training session.

(And so I am absolved.)

We take advantage of the beautiful sunshine and calm Thames waters by boating down to the Houses of Parliament. I have never crossed London by river, and the view throughout is really quite stunning. Following one of the eights, we boat past Battersea power station, several high-rise apartment buildings, old houses, new houses, penthouses. Duncan is relaxed, sitting back in the Tin Fish, which – unsurprisingly with Grant and me aboard as well – is close to taking on water. He nudges me when the London Eye and Houses of Parliament come into view.

'Being here on the Thames, coaching the Cambridge University crew – not bad for a country boy, is it?'

Grant takes a few snaps of the yellow Empacher, lit up by the sun like a candle against the background of Parliament, while the rowers take time to remove some kit and load up on electrolytes.

'I want a copy of that,' grins Duncan broadly, leaning back far enough to almost tip the Fish. 'I've deserved this after yesterday.'

CHAPTER 14

Thursday, 30 November

We meet sharply at noon, earlier than usual. The boys will be rowing a 28-kilometre stretch from Ely to Cambridge today in preparation for tomorrow's Fairbairns, a very traditional 2.9-mile race on the Cam. After founding the Head of the River Race in 1927 (which is rowed on the Championship course a week before the Boat Race and open to any crew), Jesus College rowing coach Steve Fairbairn decided that a similarly long race was needed to help his oarsmen prepare for the Lent and May bumps. Accordingly, he selected a provisional Lents line-up and raced his crews against each other over the longest distance possible on the Cam: from the Fort St George (a yellowish pub popular with rowers) to Little Bridge, a few yards beyond the A14 motorway bridge. This lock-to-lock race, also called Crock Eights, soon became a popular test of strength, and crews from Fitzwilliam, Sidney Sussex, Peterhouse and St Catharine's College asked to join in. All were, at the time, coached by Jesus oarsmen. By 1929 the race had been opened to all college crews and, based on a cup donated by Steve Fairbairn to whichever proved the fastest crew, became known from then on as the Fairbairn Cup Races.

In Ely, I join Duncan in the Tin Fish, following the eights on their two-hour journey to Cambridge. Kieran has been given the 'wing-rigger' to stroke – a shell rarely used until now, but which will be the actual boat raced against Oxford come April. Thorsten will stroke 'The Flying Welshman', a slightly older Empacher retired from the Boat Race after the customary two years and now used in the Goldie–Isis race.

There's a strong current and cold headwind today, both of which will take their toll on the oarsmen. I zip up my fleece, down jacket and Musto, lowering my head deep inside its protective collar. I trade my baseball cap for a fleece hat and put on waterproof gloves. Comfortable and warm, I park myself on one of two blue metal chairs, facing forward. Duncan's right behind me, one hand on the engine, the other clutching a megaphone. We don't say much. We can't – the engine's too noisy. Nevertheless, we seem to enjoy each other's company. I put my feet up on Bakes's metal toolkit, legs stretched, sit back and relax. The wind makes my eyes water and causes the salt to streak across my face sideways, in the direction of my ears. I wipe my cheeks dry with my gloved hand. The rough glove leaves painful marks on the skin of my face, and I make a mental note not to try that again.

Having docked at Goldie, the two crews take turns in repairing to the Captains' Room to formulate a race plan for tomorrow's Fairbairns. Competition between the crews will be fierce. The 'big four' – Thorsten, Seb, Kieran and Tom – have been split up so as to give each crew a somewhat equal share. The Empachers have each been fitted with larger rudders to help the coxswains manage the Cam's frequent and sharp turns. The rudders are long but not deep, the idea being that the eights should glide through corners, rather than cut through them.

Inevitably, not everyone gets to row tomorrow. Each of the boats seats eight oarsmen plus a coxswain, leaving four triallists on the bank. Wanne, one of those left out, is furious – at a loss to understand why Matt and Hopper should have been chosen over him. What he doesn't realise yet, of course, is that they were selected to race precisely to determine how they would cope at high ratings. Having been excluded from racing wasn't to signal his inferiority. Rather, it was the consequence of a selection experiment to tease out those unable to compete at race pace. Unable or unwilling to appreciate the difference, critical though it may be, he sulks instead, consumed by misgiving and suspicion of ulterior motives.

Back home I find the following piece of advice in my Outlook inbox:

From: Anonymous
To: Squad
Subject: Testosterone levels
Date: 30 Nov 2006 22:08:12 +0000

Hey guys,

Someone said something regarding sexual activity and levels of testosterone. Basically don't get an orgasm in the days leading up to a competition. In more detail: Several studies have been done with different time frames but the general conclusions are the same: you can get a tiny spike of testosterone before sexual activity while you are mentally aroused. During any period of abstaining from sexual activity, you can make your testosterone levels peak more greatly by becoming aroused, continuing with masturbation, and stopping during plateau, when you are maximally aroused but clear of orgasm. Doing this before competition has been demonstrated to peak testosterone levels on average of 145.7 per cent of your normal baseline for about a day after about a week of no sexual activity at all. Important to only be stimulated (without orgasm) the morning of or day of whatever competition you are competing in as your body works on negative feedback and will pull a mean trick by stopping producing awesome levels of testosterone to let them return to normal. Obtaining orgasm AFTER the competition may raise levels of 'killer cells' which theoretically should help the recovery process.

What does this mean for you? If you are up for it: Stop sexual activity. Do not look at porno or have 'private time' with your gf. Before the erg competition, watch some porn of choice (or whatever you find to be highly arousing) and do what you must do making very sure to stay clear of orgasm. In theory this will put you in a good position for having very high levels of testosterone. Stronger effort, more aggressive, more competitive, etc.

Sometime after the competition obtain orgasm via your preferred medium to up odds of faster recovery. Wash your hands before the competition.

Friday, 1 December

Today is Fairbairns. The squad meet at the usual 6:30am slot for a watered-down version of our daily dose of core muscle exercises. The two eights lie parked on trestles in the downstairs gym. Duncan announces the crew line, making it clear all the while that this is not necessarily also the line-up for Trial Eights, another selection race slated to take place in London in just over a week's time. Richard, Wanne, Barst and Marco are told to stay behind for a long row on the erg, a suggestion received rather unenthusiastically. Unsurprisingly.

With fifteen minutes to go, the boats resting expectantly on the Cam and crowds lining the riverbanks, the boys each lift an erg from the wall and line up four abreast for a warm-up session. I borrow a bicycle and join the coaches on the towpath, from where we will cycle along with one of the crews. Kieran's eight is the first to take off, pushing hard to get up to speed, past Elizabeth Way Bridge and off around the corner into the distance. But it's Thorsten's crew that seize the day, finishing a good 28 seconds ahead of Kieran's. As the crews lie panting past the finish line, Thorsten motions for me to come over.

'How did we do?' he breathes excitedly.

'Pretty good. You had 28 seconds on Kieran.'

Thorsten punches the air. That'll be two-nil in his favour when it comes to stroke seat selection, and he knows it. For them, the real battle is not for a seat in the Blue Boat – which is more or less a given in their cases – but for the chance at that most prestigious of seats: to stroke the eight. Needless to say, Kieran is terribly disappointed, his hands holding his head as he stares glumly at his footplate. Seb, sitting right behind him, is furious, ploughing his fist violently into the muddy riverbank while letting everyone in the crew have a piece of his mind. The rest of the crew remain there silently, letting Germany's fury drift by like a dark cloud.

Kieran's crew had gone off too hard, and were unable to sustain this pace for the duration of the race and settle into a comfortable rhythm. Their keenness to impress got the better of them, though racing experience should have told them otherwise. After all, one of the benefits of experience is the ability to pace oneself throughout a race.

Be that as it may, it remains tough to lose, tougher even to get back on your feet. The price of glory is not just the physical pain – the mind-numbing erg sessions, the perpetual fatigue and dieting, the blisters, cracked hands and festering sores, the coughs and colds that drag on endlessly, the unhappy girlfriends. It also entails psychological injury – the necessary shame of defeat, always public, without the reassurance that ultimately all will be well, that soap and warm showers and hot chocolate are ready and waiting for those who give it all. That honour will ultimately come to all who deserve it. Because it doesn't always, does it? It's knowing that a happy ending is not to be had by all – this is the terrible toll exacted for the possibility, not probability, of success.

Monday, 4 December

Me (whispering): '*Damn*—'

I freeze in my tracks, midway down the thick-carpeted winding staircase. The burglar alarm is going berserk, its high-pitch whine drowning out anything and everything else at this early morning hour. I, meanwhile, feel sick to my stomach. I listen out for the dogs. There are three of them, all Huskies the size of Saint Bernards and extraordinarily protective of owner and property. I recall last night's conversation over dinner, about Huskies being instinctive and close to their primordial wolf-like nature, and that they enjoy catching birds – these three in particular – and that when they do they tear them to shreds, alive but unable to stop their limbs being ripped off. The description left nothing to the imagination. It didn't do much for my appetite either.

My heart's in my throat, the hair on my arms raised. Is that the sound of dogs running up the stairs?

I couldn't have been happier seeing Marco, dressed in striped pyjamas, bouncing down the flights of stairs and on towards the plastic console that controls the burglar alarm. With practised movements he gags the sirens and peace returns to the Espin household.

'Sorry about the alarm ...'

'No worries, man.' Marco smiles and he climbs back up the stairs. 'Help yourself to some breakfast. There's cereal in the cupboard, there's orange juice, bread, milk, toast, whatever – take what you like. I'll be down soon too.'

Marco is once again host to several of us without a London address while training on the Tideway. The plan calls for a week's training in preparation for Trial Eights – an annual affair that sees two Cambridge crews of about equal strength race each other over the Boat Race course. It's an unusually important component of the training and selection programme for both Cambridge and Oxford. Naturally, there will be keen interest by Oxford in our Trial Eights – as, indeed, there is from our side in theirs. The squad, no doubt, will want to size up the competition. It's the first time either crew will race the full course under race conditions. Our Trial Eights is slated for Friday; Oxford will race its two crews a day earlier. And so this week the 2007 Oxford and Cambridge crews will meet informally on the riverbank for the very first time. Oxford boats from Westminster School's boathouse, just four doors down from KCS. And yet miles apart in so many other ways.

The Tideway is a name given to that section of the Thames subject to tides. This stretch of water, home to most of London's rowing clubs, is just short of 100 miles in length, extending downstream from Teddington Lock (the highest point in the tidal Thames) to the North Sea.* This tide rises and falls twice a day by anything

---

*As an aside, James Behren, President of the legendary 1993 Cambridge crew, was nicknamed Teddington because 'the tide turns at Teddington', a metaphor for Cambridge finally turning the tables on their arch-rival after having won only one of the previous seventeen races.

up to 7m (24ft) and takes longer to flow out (between six and nine hours) than it does to flow in (four to five hours). It's known to take visitors by surprise, many not realising that what looks like a docile stream in the early morning swells by a good few metres in the space of several hours. Particularly for those parked on the sloping concrete dock (popular with rowers and unsuspecting tourists), the tidal river can be hazardous, occasionally plundering the dock of parked cars, providing sufficient buoyancy for them to be carried downstream, or to be dispatched entirely as they sink below the water line. Even for those successful at rescuing their vehicle, the water leaves a terrible stench, a sugary residue of effluent and human waste that is nearly impossible to eradicate.

As Duncan and I allow ourselves to drift leisurely in the Tin Fish with the incoming tide while waiting for one of the eights to reappear from underneath Putney Bridge, an animated Donald comes rushing at us at full speed, Grant operating the outboard motor. Donald gestures frantically. They pull up alongside us.

Donald: 'Your car is about to float away!'

Duncan (cupping his right ear): 'Sorry?'

Donald and Grant (together): 'YOUR CAR IS ABOUT TO FLOAT AWAY!'

Duncan: '*Shit* ...'

This is followed by a command for me to 'hold on' while Duncan revs the engine and, at full speed, heads straight back in the direction of the boathouses. My eyes water in the headwind as we speed across the river. I peer into the distance. There, some 300 yards up the road from the boathouses, I spot the top half of what appears to be a red Citroën with all lights flashing.

'Shit, shit, shit! Shit! The electrics have gone. That's not good – *not* good.'

Duncan pulls the Fish up to the grey metal railing separating his car and us, and clambers across it only to sink up to his thighs in the murky brown Thames. He wades the nine or so feet to his now mostly-submerged vehicle and unlocks the driver's door. The water level inside near enough covers the dashboard. Duncan, more generous than usual with profanities and without giving it a second thought, sits down in the puddle that was his driver's seat, and attempts to start the car. To my surprise (and I expect his too), the engine coughs a couple of times and starts, allowing him to slowly edge it up the sloping road to safety on higher ground. There was no repeat of the engine starting for at least the next two days.

'That's 400 quid down the bloody drain,' he says glumly as he climbs back in the launch, everything below the waistline soaked to the bone.

Having regained the basics of composure, Duncan drives the Fish back to Putney Bridge in time to see Kieran's wing-rigger speed past. In the distance, Thorsten's eight is approaching. Their rowing looks much lighter and longer than Kieran's and also much less aggressive. Rowing, when done well, looks almost lazy – deceptively so – with light but quick catches, blades filled upon entry, and power applied consistently throughout the stroke. It's beautiful to watch. Despite this, however, Kieran's crew were in fact faster over the Boat Race course by a good 20 seconds. It's an interesting reversal of fortunes, and a useful reminder that the most elegant row need not also be the fastest.

Duncan, Donald, Bakes and Grant sit down to decide a line-up for Trial Eights. Wanne will be relieved to know that he's included. So will Hopper. Matt, alas, is out, and takes this as his cue to bin himself. As a Harvard medical student on a one-year Masters course, he has concluded that he's far too busy to continue training at this rate. He's the third triallist so far to have eliminated himself. To press the self-destruct button may have left them with at least a small degree of dignity – a sense of control, or the mere appearance of it, over their own destinies. Perhaps some of the toll paid for Boat Race glory (or any achievement in sports) is the potential cost to one's self-esteem, the risk of one's sense of self being dented by rejection. To that extent, 'self-binning' is just damage-limitation, even if deplorable by CUBC standards.

Friday, 8 December

Trial Eight crews just announced. The first boat (aptly called 'Stay Calm') is to be stroked by Thorsten with, behind him, David Hopper, Tobias Garnett, Jacob Cornelius, Alastair MacLeod, Tom James, Colin Scott and Kip McDaniel, with Rebecca Dowbiggin at the rudder. The second ('Just Relax') will have Kieran West at stroke and comprises David Billings, Dan O'Shaughnessy, Wanne Kromdijk, Oliver de Groot, Pete Champion, Don Wyper and Sebastian Schulte, with Russ Glenn as coxswain. The crews are due on the water at 10:30. I join Bakes in the Tin Fish for a short pre-race outing: a paddle up to Hammersmith Bridge and three 15-stroke bursts on the way back to the boathouse, followed by two practice starts. Kieran's crew have come a long way since their Fairbairns defeat. Their catches are lighter, their strokes longer and more controlled, their recoveries more relaxed, their rowing more rhythmic overall. Bakes expresses great confidence in what has become 'his' crew, at least for the week leading up to Trial Eights, and he tells the boys this repeatedly. After all, he says, for the crew to know that the coach has confidence in them is extremely important.

Ever since the crews were announced, the guys have kept to their own. Duncan has taken a step back as Head Coach and handed the reins to Bakes and Grant, the latter charged with Thorsten's crew. To physically separate the crews is good practice for the Boat Race, where the boys will be facing a competitor they know little or nothing about, other than the wash-ups and broadsheet speculations. Thus the crews will take their lunches separately, train separately, debrief separately and socialise separately for the week – allowing each to create an identity of its own. Looking at them now, it's clear that a significant amount of tension has already built up between the crews, each protective of its own interests, thinking itself superior, yet keen to glean whatever information can be gathered on the other crew too. This is of course no different from the actual Boat Race, where both Cambridge and Oxford will go to considerable lengths to speculate on what each other's tactics might be. Different tactics are required depending on whether one starts at the Surrey or Middlesex station, even if both crews will cover the exact same distance. Middlesex has the advantage of the first bend past Fulham football stadium that, in real terms, is worth the equivalent of a quarter length of a boat. The objective for the crew starting on Middlesex would be to use that bend to their advantage so as to get ahead of the other crew somewhere around Harrods' Depository and before Hammersmith Bridge. Generally speaking, a strong tide should benefit the crew racing on the Middlesex side of the river. That said, the precise point in the river where the tidal stream is strongest can vary considerably from day to day. The Surrey station, on the other hand, confers the distinct advantage of rowing on the inside of the long Surrey bend (which begins at about Hammersmith Bridge). This bend is worth a full boat length and has the added advantage of some shelter from the wind in the wider reaches of the river. The latter can be particularly beneficial if a strong wind blows directly against the tide and the water beyond Hammersmith turns menacing. Only once a crew is sufficiently far ahead of its competitor (usually at least half a boat length) can it move safely over onto the other station so as to try to gain whatever advantages the remainder of the course has in store. The final bend around Barnes Bridge favours Middlesex by three-quarters of a length.

The objective is pretty clear for either crew: to get ahead before Hammersmith Bridge (not since 1997 has a Middlesex crew out-rowed their Surrey-based competitor in the outside bend when lagging behind). Even so, there are different ways of accomplishing this objective. Should one blast off the start even if this risks having fewer reserves left at later stages in the race? Or should one prioritise settling into a sustainable rhythm as soon as possible, even if that risks lagging behind slightly early in the race? A fast start can of course earn the crew that slight, but crucial, psychological edge. Where and at what point should the coxswain call for a mighty push? Does one approach the race as a single seventeen-minute piece or tackle it in stages instead?

Last night, Bakes circulated a tried-and-tested pre-race routine (which seems to have originated with a former Goldie rower):

Pre-Race Routine
Ovaltine Lite before bed
Sleep well, 8 hours + earplugs
Breakfast – Weetabix/brown toast and honey, glass of Beroca
Shit and shower (last min cold)
Morning – walk/stretch
Think about the race, my role, the crew focus
Listen to pre-race music – go through each part of race in head
Imagine the crew rowing well – picture the best performances to date
Piss/shit, kit/water
Crew chat and race plan
Be clear about how to respond to changing conditions:
    Tail – quick pick up, spring off and finishes held not pulled
    Head – defined catches, grip up and dynamic swing
    through to finishes held high
Relax into the warm-up: concentrate on rowing well, ignore the surroundings – our bubble
Check everything – twice
On the start do not look at opponents – our race plan and our technical focus
Breathe deep, feel the rhythm you want – picture going off the start. Do it.
Execute the race plan and send out a message to Isis and the Blue Boat: 'We are a serious unit and we're not fucking around.'
Finish with no regrets

It's interesting to see crews mentally prepare for a race. Don, in a fashion befitting his brash nature, saps adrenaline from fight scenes on celluloid. He's claimed a seat on an old cloth sofa opposite me, MacBook on his knees, watching the introductory scene to *Rocky IV*. Its familiar 'Eye of the Tiger' theme song reverberates throughout the small, spartan room, though that's of no concern to Don. His eyes remain intently focused on the plasma screen in front, his mind oblivious to those around him. His effort is in earnest. For him, there's a war on and he's a soldier. It's kill or be killed.

Dan sits next to Don, trying hard to concentrate on a book but distracted by Don's theatrics. Seb sits opposite (and next to me), faring likewise with a thick paperback, and on my other side, philosopher Dave Billings is engrossed in Wright's *A Short History of Progress*. Bakes fiddles nervously with his Nokia.

With five minutes to go until the coin toss, Bakes calls us over to the tall glass doors facing the Tideway. He explains that there seems to be a lot of land water flowing into the river and that the stream today is likely to be quite wide. The start and first six minutes up to Harrods' Depository, he says, will be crucial and, given this, he would opt for Middlesex if given the choice. He asks for our feedback. The boys, however, remain quiet. Earlier this morning they all felt strongly in favour of the Surrey station – often preferred for its long bend – but so close to the race it looks as if they prefer not to have to focus on anything other than racing, and are happy for Bakes, or anyone, to make this decision for them. The mind only copes with so much pressure. As it happens, our crew lose the coin toss and get saddled with Middlesex.

I barter myself a seat on one of the traditional wooden launches, hired specifically for this purpose. The launch is full of Old Blues drawn together by their shared commitment to help Cambridge win this year's Boat Race. There are a total of five launches following the Trial Eights: two Tin Fishes and three antiques – one for the umpire, one for the press, and one for the Blues. I make myself comfortable on one of the wooden benches that line the stern of the boat and, together with the eleven or so others present, stare into the distance for a first glimpse of the crews. They soon appear from underneath Putney Bridge and row up to the starting line (formally referred to as the University Stone) where they wait for the umpire's command.

Once the eights are lined up and the coxswains have lowered their arms to indicate their crews are ready, the umpire raises his flag and calls for 'Attention …', followed by a decisive 'GO!' The crews are quick off the mark. Thorsten takes the rating up to an impressive 44 strokes per minute and, as a result, takes a half-length advantage even before the Black Buoy (a well-known landmark on the Championship course at about a minute-and-a-half into the race). We follow at a safe distance, our eyes glued all the while to the yellow shells pulling away from us. The race is an exciting one to watch. Even if Thorsten's crew never surrendered its early advantage, Kieran's put up a good fight, gaining on its rival three times during the race, once even in the Surrey bend from the Middlesex station. The Old Blues seem pleased and it's *rah rah* all round.

On our way back to Cambridge, Rebecca takes a call on her mobile, wondering whether any of us would like to hear what the broadsheets will be saying about our performance today. But of course we would. I turn down the volume on the car stereo. Rebecca repeats, in half-sentence chunks, the press release as relayed to her by phone:[17]

The high winds and rough water that tested Oxford's Trial race yesterday abated enough to allow an excellent race between Cambridge's two crews – 'Stay Calm', stroked by German World Champion Thorsten Engelmann, and 'Just Relax', led by Sydney gold medallist Kieran West.

'Stay Calm', steered by Rebecca Dowbiggin, took an early lead off the start with President Tom James, Canadian international Kristopher (Kip) McDaniel and Colin Scott providing a powerful engine room behind the experienced 25-year-old Engelmann.

By the Black Buoy, two minutes into the race, they had a

length and looked set to row away from their opponents but, on the corner at Fulham, West hit back as Dowbiggin took her crew wide, allowing her rival Russell Glenn, last year's Goldie cox, back into the race.

With a second German World Champion, Sebastian Schulte, American Don Wyper and Peter Champion behind him, West mounted attack after attack, repeatedly closing the gap, but Engelmann was always able to respond and hold on to his advantage. At Hammersmith Bridge, reached in seven minutes ten seconds, they were four seconds ahead.

As the crews passed St Paul's School, Glenn steered his crew over towards the Surrey side and at St Paul's the crews had swapped stations, with the crews almost overlapping. But again Engelmann stayed calm and moved out again to lead by two lengths at Barnes Bridge. Glenn's crew continued to fight back and had reduced the deficit at the finish to just four seconds.

Cambridge have a strong squad and today's display will reinforce the opinion of many experts that they are, on paper, the pre-Race favourites.

'The Boat Race is all about what happens on the day,' said coach Duncan Holland after the race. 'The Race is no respecter of reputations. We know that Oxford will have a good crew.'

Holland has been preparing his crews without the normal side-by-side racing in the week leading up to today's race. 'In an Olympic final you have a good idea of your opposition because you will have seen them racing on the circuit,' he said. 'But on the Boat Race day your opposition is an unknown. We wanted to replicate that.'

'It was a pretty positive build-up for us,' agreed Tom James, the Cambridge President who was in the winning crew. 'It meant we came to the race fresh and it was a tough race. They kept attacking and attacking and we had to continually fight them off and we never had more than a quarter length of clear water throughout the race.'

The evening is concluded in traditional fashion with a Trial Eights Dinner, useful not least in helping to patch up affairs between the two crews. After Fairbairns and Trial Eights, where the squad is divided so as to mimic Boat Race conditions, it's crucial to bring both crews together into a coherent squad with a single objective: to beat Oxford.

CHAPTER 15

Tuesday, 19 December

Today's 5-kilometre erg test marks the end of the pre-Christmas training period. It's the first of two 5-k races, designed to test for power and endurance. In some ways these are far more useful than the popular 2,000-metre test. After all, the Boat Race takes place over a course of 4 miles and 374 yards (nearly 7 kilometres). By contrast, most international races (including the Olympic Games and World Championships) are only 2 kilometres in length. Small, square electronic displays stick out like periscopes from the Concept II ergometers and keep track of a variety of useful measures. They help the oarsman know where he is during the race and whether he's on or off target, and allow the coaches to gain an accurate read-out of the deterioration of power over the virtual 5-kilometre race course.

Pre-race anxiety set in several days ago. Everyone knows this is one of the more important selection criteria and is keen to do well. Aside from some practice runs over 1,500 metres during the early morning erg sessions last week, the boys are careful to eat well and sleep a lot. This morning they will have risen early – some as early as 5:00am – to get their bodies woken up and alert for the 9:30am race.

At a couple of minutes past eight, the first few wander in to stretch and warm up, in no mood for conversation. There is none of the usual chattering and faffing about. Nor is there any sense of collectivity or team spirit. Today's test is about individual performance: a struggle for survival of the individual pitted against the squad. Needless to say, the atmosphere is suspenseful; pregnant with anticipation. No one particularly wants to do this. At the same time, they are keen to see how they will fare after three months of intense physical exercising. They think relationally. They each come equipped with a sense of whereabouts they rank within the squad and what numbers they will need to lay down today to improve, or at least maintain, their status – a judgement based on their recent performance at the Indoor Championship, on feedback from the coaches (albeit always non-committal), and their everyday performance on the ergs, weights and water. This self-assessment is ongoing and something the athletes, regardless of experience, are extremely sensitive to. After all, every erg session, every weights session, every water session produces data – vast reams of which are kept and pored over endlessly by Duncan and his assistant coaches – but not all of which are made public. This forces the boys to keep a mental record of what they remember, or imagine, someone else may or may not have done, and what this might mean for their own standing within the squad. Individual performances have an effect on everyone else in the squad, as if their identities were woven into a single cloth. Movements in one outpost invariably have an effect on the others. It is as Berkeley professor Judith Butler suspected: one does not 'do' status alone, but is always 'doing' it with or for another, even if the other is only imaginary. What I might call my own status or identity may appear as something that I authored or indeed own. Nothing is further from the truth. The terms that make up one's own status or identity are, from the start, outside oneself – in a sociality that has no single author. Status, like identity, is a collective enterprise, it's something you do together, something acquired not in a vacuum but in the company of others.

Today will show whether the rankings accumulated to date are justified. Any doubts around these contribute to the earnestness of this wintry morning. Besides, today's results will determine who will stay and who will go. Those allowed to stay will join the squad for their winter training in Banyoles, northern Spain. This ten-day camp is ordinarily used to arrive at a preliminary selection for Goldie and the Blue Boat. Banyoles' tranquil, green, 2-kilometre lake provides near-perfect conditions for seat-racing. The rowing lake, and the small unassuming town surrounding it, gained international fame when selected as one of the venues for the 1992 Barcelona Olympics. Not knowing whether they will be invited to accompany the squad to Spain can be extremely unsettling for those in the lower half of the squad. Those deemed viable candidates for either Goldie or the Blue Boat will be told to pack their bags and come along, meaning they might have to travel back to Cambridge (sometimes from as far away as Canada or the US) more or less immediately after having finished their Christmas pudding, to join the squad on 27 December for ten days of training and racing.

In the gym, meanwhile, Groove Armada's 'I See You Baby' drones on in the background, ill at ease with the solemnity of this early pre-test hour. The boys pace the boathouse nervously or lie flat, to stretch their long stiff limbs.

Seven Concept IIs are lined up and waiting patiently on the green rubber floor. With only fifteen minutes to go, the boys strap their feet into the ergs for a series of short trial runs. As usual, Russ, the coxswain, oscillates between the triallists, jotting down their various race plans in his notebook. These notes will help him coach the guys during the test. Though their plans differ slightly, many of them will try to settle down at a steady rating and split for the first 2,000 metres and then to 'negative split' the next 3,000. I station myself between Wanne and Ali, both of whom will aim for a steady 1:38.

Duncan calls the race with his usual 'Cambridge. Attention? Go!' At Go, Russ cranks up the volume as the guys sprint off the starting lines. Jake, Kip and Pete have pushed their splits below 1:35. Wanne and Ali have settled at 1:37. As soon as any of their splits drop below those predicted in their race plan, Russ rallies them, stringing together half-sentences of moral support: 'Bring it down now – that's a good one – on the legs – swing – keep breathing – keep it strong – keep fighting – you know what you've got to do ...' Then, when all is finally over after five gruelling kilometres, the athletes let go of the handle and flop sideways off the erg and onto the rubber floor, exhausted, wet with perspiration, their lips turned blue for lack of oxygen. Some are worse affected than others. The ginger-haired British junior international Doug Perrin has retreated to the back of the gym with a black plastic bin cupped between his knees. His already pale skin is now translucent. He pukes up violently.

Jake, likewise, has been busy spring-cleaning after a formidable 15:40 tally. I find him in the changing room, on the floor with his back against the wall, facing a urinal. The urinal is lined with a greyish, mortar-like substance.

'I think I'll go use the other lavatory,' Hopper mutters drily, his head appearing then disappearing around the corner. Jake manages a weak smile. 'I'll just pee over it and it'll be gone.' The urinal, however, no longer drains properly and as I flush it, it overflows, making a messy situation rather a lot worse.

The test done and dusted, and with the last batch of athletes strewn about like damp rags, Duncan announces the results. On top came Thorsten with a stunning 15:11 and Seb at 15:25. To give you some idea of how impressive these results are, the British–Irish record set by Olympic gold medallist James Cracknell stands at 15:09.9. 'Oh, and everyone's coming to Banyoles,' says Duncan, smirking at the obvious relief of those at the bottom end of the twenty-strong squad. That said, we each leave for our Christmas holidays.

Leaving Goldie is like stepping from one all-consuming world into another, and my first reaction is that of a nauseating boredom. My ordinary world seems strangely void without the regimented training, the perpetual tiredness and mood swings. Email traffic between the oarsmen, normally pretty lively, has come to a halt too, except for one message from Russ.

From: Russ Glenn
To: R.M. Dowbiggin
Cc: Squad
Subject: Merry Christmas
Date: Sun, 24 Dec 2006 23:06:26 -0500

Merry Christmas!

I hope all of you have had a wonderful holidays thus far, and a fantastic Christmas day ahead.

I read something today that I figured I'd share:

I remember seeing a TV interview with Daley Thompson during his reign, where he was asked by the interviewer how he managed to always stay ahead of his great rival. His response really had an impact on me and has always stuck in my mind. He said, 'It's quite easy really. I train harder than he does. I know, for example, that he will not be training on Christmas day, so I make sure I do. One day's extra training might just be the difference between coming first and second.'

I don't really know who Thompson was, or why he was apparently the best decathlete ever, but he seems to have been one hard son of a bitch. That's pretty much all I wanted to share. I know y'all aren't training stupidly over the holidays, but though Banyoles is coming up let's remember that it's not only about selection in Jan, but about crushing Oxford come April – with the same single minded focus that Thompson showed.

My thoughts are with y'all through the holidays,

r

CHAPTER 16

Friday, 29 December

Ventured out into the crisp morning air and across the damp common that separates our home from the carnival of boathouses that line one bank of the River Cam. Between these and almost straight ahead is The Goldie, its Cambridge blue barn doors a lid on the hundreds of ergo miles dispatched since September. All is eerily quiet on the common save for one solitary someone, listless dog in tow.

It's just gone seven. Looking at the gloominess of it all, it's nice to think that in a few hours' time we'll be in northern Spain, in a small town renowned for hosting one of the world's best regatta courses, cupped between green hills, and behind them snowcapped mountains. It's here that selection decisions will be made and a provisional Blue Boat crew decided upon. Needless to say, tensions are bound to rise well beyond anything seen so far this season. Spirits will be lifted and broken, and friendships tested, as twenty of the boys compete for eight seats in the only boat that matters.

A popular technique for separating wheat from chaff in Boat Race selection is 'seat-racing'. The principle behind it is relatively straightforward. Two coxed fours of similar strength and ability race each other under the same conditions at a capped rating (of, say, 32 strokes per minute) over a straight 1,500-metre course. Coxswains are only allowed to call the rating and distance, and must refrain from giving technical instructions or encouragement.

After the first race, two rowers will be told to swap places, one from each crew, after which the boats will race each other again over the same distance at the same rating, so as to try to isolate the effect of one rower on a crew. This exercise gives coaches a reasonably good indication of someone's boat-moving ability – for what matters of course is not absolute speed but the difference in speed between the boats (or the impact of changing one rower on boat speed). And so the process continues, each time with two new rowers swapping places, one from each crew. The nature of seat-racing is such that rowers have no choice but to oscillate between friend and foe, working flawlessly with the very same people they're in competition with. Often, the fastest boat movers are not also necessarily the most powerful individuals as measured at indoor tests (though the very best oarsmen like Steve Redgrave, Mahe Drysdale and Andy Hodge will be both strong on the ergs and technically superior). These are the men able to move boats well beyond what anyone would predict, given their profile on paper. All that matters, after all, is the ability to move a boat fast over the Championship course – a feat that is at once intensely personal yet leaves no scope whatever for individual expression.

The beauty of seat-racing as a selection tool is that it allows coaches to look at rowers in combination – to study the impact of various combinations on the water. To that extent, competitive rowing becomes a *combinatorial* game – a matter of finding the fastest mix of individuals – which is a quite different thing from totting up the fastest individual oarsmen. And, frankly, this process is as intuitive as it is scientific, as subjective as it is objective, leaving ample scope for insecurity and confusion on the part of the athletes.

'Hey, this is an appropriate passage.' Russ lies sprawled out across our nuptial arrangement, browsing my battered copy of Halberstam's rowing classic, *The Amateurs*.

'What is?'
Russ, legs crossed, reads:

If rowing was an estimable sport filled with virtue and honour and strength, then there was something about the team camps that was the reverse of that. They became its Darwinian lowest common denominator. This camp was, if anything, worse; it was filled with anxiety and tension that turned inevitably into paranoia. So much depended on so little that was quantifiable.

'Sums it up really, doesn't it?', I reply.

Our first few days at camp are spent at a rather unimaginative hotel some 500 yards from the rowing lake. Most of us share double rooms. Tom's assigned me Room 105 to share with Russ, a hardy yet good-humoured American doctoral student and veteran of two successful Goldie races. This season is to be his big break into Blue Boat territory and things are looking up. He is by far the more experienced of the two remaining trial coxswains. The room, nine by twelve feet, features two single beds pushed together as if to craft a makeshift double bed, and, on each side, a small bedside table.

Neither of us is man enough to move the beds apart. Instead we stare at the sleeping arrangement with curiosity, reluctant to broach the subject, and instead get on with unpacking our belongings. The floor is a sterile white tiled marble. The walls, also a dull white, sport three small gold-framed pictures, torn it seems from some travel magazine. The pink bedcovers hide an uncomfortable, thin foam mattress, about two inches in height, and beneath it a grey iron frame.

Our anti-climactic lodgings are compensated for by a cloudless deep blue sky and, underneath it, a green lake. Duncan charges the boys with a run around the lake while we unload the trailer. The 24-hour trailer ride from Cambridge to northern Spain has left its mark on the boats – the otherwise yellow Empachers are covered in greasy black soot from continuous exposure to diesel fumes. Upon arrival at the boatsheds, however, the place is deserted and the entrance closed.

'They're so fucking poorly organised here,' complains Donald, 'they couldn't organise a piss-up in a brewery.'

Duncan ventures out to try to find someone awake at this siesta hour so we can get on with our job.

As we move the last single into the boatshed, we can see our athletes return from their run in a single line on the narrow tow-path, snaking their way back to the hotel and straight into the showers. We too, covered in soot from handling the boats, opt for freshening up before beers.

Donald is buying.

CHAPTER 17

That night I find myself in a classroom not quite like my teaching rooms in Cambridge but a little like them, and in it are my work colleagues, managing to pull off what must be the worst presentation ever. The crowd is getting restless, as I am, about the total lack of empathy on the part of my peers, and I decide to make a stand and march out angrily into a dark hallway leading to a holiday flat somewhere in Spain; and as I come walking in, Roxana comes walking out of the apartment pushing a pram with a newborn inside it. Must be mine, I think, but I have no recollection of making or anticipating it.

The apartment is cloaked in twilight, the air not yet advanced to complete darkness, but it soon will be – and it all feels rather ominous. I switch on the lights in one room, but while this solves one problem it creates another, as the other rooms in the apartment now look even more inhospitable than they already did. I'm conscious of something dark moving behind me – not a person but the shadow of one. I freeze. The apartment, however, is eerily quiet. My heart, beating rapidly, has sought solace at the back of my throat. There's no one in this room but me. The adrenaline surges through my system, veins throbbing noisily in my head …

I wake up feeling queasy, roused by 'my own moan, a moan caused by a big roaring Whoo Whoo in my head that had shot me out of my pillow like a ghost'.[18] Around me images lie scattered, a dream defrocked for the delusion it is, but not therefore less visible or less real. Must we, I wonder, lop off these manifestations of the spirit in the interest of detachment and objectivity? Will that make my account of time spent with the squad more objective, more true? Or are dreams, like Pullman's daemons, unable to exist at significant distances from us without incurring great pain?

My T-shirt is sickly damp and my temperature's searing. My heartbeat's where I left it last, making it difficult to breathe except in short spurts. The blanket's half on the bed and half off it. I look to my right where Russ is fast asleep, impervious to my moaning, curled up like an infant, facing the window and, beyond that, the dark night outside. Can he really still be asleep, I wonder? Is he being polite by pretending to be asleep when all this racket was going on? I gaze at him sleepily.

CHAPTER 18

Saturday, 30 December

Cool stone stairs descend into a room nicely laid out with colourful foodstuffs: cereals, croissants, cheese, meats, yoghurt, fruit, coffee and tea, jams. Everyone already there pretty much rolled straight out of bed, crumpled faces buried beneath a cap or beanie.

The first lot of eight athletes take off at half past seven to rig two coxed fours and paddle out onto the lake. I join them on their short walk to where the boats are stored. The weather outside is cold but refreshing too – the lake extraordinarily beautiful: calm, composed and protected by a film of translucent mist. At first the pontoons seem to be coated in thin layers of early morning frost, and I think how chilly it must be to stand there bare-footed, as the boys will shortly. But striding across them I realise they are constructed out of a white plastic. It makes for a nice contrast to the green underneath. I continue walking, peering deeply into the water and able to see the sandy bottom for the first ten or so feet before it tumbles into an abyss. As with most mountain lakes, it's deep, dark, cold. Standing at the very end, and with my back against the snow-capped mountains, I make out stone huts scattered in a semi-circle around the lake, the functions of which aren't entirely clear to me. They're far too small to live in, yet they speak of times past, of tea parties and gentry and old money and debauchery and drunkenness at night.

As the first lot take their rigged fours onto the cold white pontoons and gently into the water, the rest of the boys arrive and get down to washing and rigging two eights, two coxless fours, two pairs, and two singles. By the time the first lot finish their row, the second is done, changed, warmed up, and keen too to sample the lake.

❖

Back at the hotel, I join Duncan outside in the sunshine.

'Here you go—'

I hand Duncan a glass of Spanish draught. There are, after all, few things tastier than an ice-cold beer after an afternoon of hard labour.

'Cheers.'

We sit talking on cheap white garden furniture, the setting a small patio between the hotel and the road next to it. Behind us someone's lit up, spoiling the late afternoon air with the harsh, sinister reek of cigarette smoke.

'Selection's a damn difficult thing to do,' Duncan muses.

He leans back in his white plastic chair pensively, looking not at me but into the street where a car has just come purring past. I look over at him, at this gruff, bearded, bald, bespectacled New Zealander who, in a former life, worked his way around the islands as a jack-of-all-trades – shearing sheep and slaughtering them, felling and stripping trees, building houses, doing whatever paid the bills wherever he happened to be at the time – just so he could afford to continue rowing competitively. In that respect things have changed little. Rowing still is an amateur pursuit with few if any material rewards. He entered Lincoln University, New Zealand, as a mature student and left with a good Bachelor of Commerce degree in economics and statistics. An avowed atheist, he cares deeply for rowing and for 'his boys', making it unfortunate (though not at all unusual for sports coaches who were once competitive athletes themselves) that his people skills don't quite live up to his superb technical skills. He is, after all, an alpha male, as they are.

His career cut short by a nasty back injury, Duncan took up coaching instead. He takes particular pride in a 'positive' approach – one that unlike much traditional coaching focuses not on finding fault but on finding occasions for positive reinforcement. Rowers, more than anyone else, are desperate for the boat to sit and move fast. They are, after all, on the receiving end of a bad row. With selection looming larger with every new day, Duncan is acutely aware that disappointing some of the Blue Boat borderlines – like Jake, Dan, Don, Colin or Oli – as he invariably must, is likely to generate resentment in Goldie, as indeed it did last year. Rather than fortifying the Blue Boat by providing it with a strong but supportive training partner, Goldie sought to undermine its bigger brother at every opportunity – or so it felt to the Blue Boat crew – creating much loathing between the crews.

The problem of course is that, of this year's Blue Boat, four seats are pretty much earmarked already by the 'big four' – the two German World Champions, Thorsten and Seb, the former Olympic gold medallist Kieran West, and the technically superb Tom James – leaving just four seats in the bow up for grabs. Competing for the two stroke-side seats are the brusque Dartmouth boy Wyper, the Canadian international O'Shaughnessy and fellow Brits Oli and Colin. Contending for the vacancies on the bow side are the blond, curly-haired dentist Pete Champion, the American Jake Cornelius, Harvard stroke Kip McDaniel, and philosopher Dave Billings. Seeing that Jake is ambidextrous, he is able to compete for a seat on stroke side as well, should Pete prove himself man enough to equal Jake's formidable power.

Sunday, 31 December

Sauntering into the breakfast room this morning accompanied by the smells of freshly brewed coffee and citrus fruit, one can cut the tension with a knife. Personal space comes at a premium today: the boys act like grumpy bears, their caps pulled down and iPods turned up, the usual chatter gone, even the occasional fart failing to invite the customary mockery. I pour myself a black coffee, grab a yoghurt, a croissant, slice of cheese and some strawberry jam, and sit down at one of the small, white-topped tables. I make one or two half-hearted attempts at conversation before allowing myself the luxury of being swept up in the earnestness of it all.

Pete, Colin, Oli, Don, Dan and Kip will be seat-raced this morning. For every single one of them, today's performance matters, weighing heavily in favour of either a Blue Boat seat or one in Goldie. Ruling out Hopper because of a sore wrist, Wanne because of a cold, and Ali who's recovering from a chest infection, only genuine Blue Boat contenders will be seat-raced today.

Two fours lie, guts-up, facing the boatshed like yellow coffins on trestles. The guys take turns fiddling with the rigging, adjusting footplates, inspecting seats, checking and double-checking the tightness of nuts. I meanwhile hoist myself up on an old oil barrel, filled to the brim with concrete and allowing me a nice vantage point from which to absorb the unfolding scene. As the time for racing draws near, the boys and coaches group together for a final debriefing. Aside from the usual words of encouragement, Duncan supplies the necessary instructions: after a short 4,000-metre warm-up row, both fours are to line up at the second red buoy, a full 500 metres into the race course.

Bakes, Grant, Linda and I are to make our way to a purpose-built, two-storey tower at the far end of the green lake, to take down finishing times. Constructed out of hardwood, the tower features an enclosed umpire cabin, protected from the elements by four full-length glass windows, and a small patio one floor up providing a 360-degree view over the lake and surrounding area. From on top, the view is breathtaking.

By the time we get there, the sun has warmed up the air so that our breath no longer shows against the faultless morning sky. The tower's simple and beautiful structure soars proudly over a shallow swamp, on stilts. The reeds surrounding it are tall too, and nearly within reach of the cabin. Fumbling with my clipboard while taking in the view, I drop my biro, which greets the muddy waters with a soft but definitive plop.

Howard Guest

6:30am: the day begins with a long erg session.

Howard Guest

Canadian Dan O'Shaughnessy during his 5k erg test.

Tom James, CUBC President, 2006–07.

Howard Guest

Howard Guest

Duncan Holland, chief coach.

Howard Guest

Stanford oarsman Jake Cornelius during an early-morning erg session.

Mark de Rond

Grant Craies, assistant coach.

The American Russ Glenn, hoping to cox the Blue Boat.

The author watching the Goldie crew at work on the ergs.

Returning to the Ely boathouse as evening falls on the River Great Ouse.

Phil Searle

Donald Legget and Rob Baker on a coaching launch.

Howard Guest

Phil Searle

The Canadian Kip McDaniel resting his sore back.

Sophie Pickford (www.sophiepickford.com)

Rebecca Dowbiggin.

Tom James and Robin Ejsmond-Frey (OUBC President) and the infamous dolphin.

The Blue Boat.

Having passed the University Post ahead of Oxford.

Lifting the coveted trophy.

Bakes, smirking, hands me another.

Grant and Rob take turns in supplying a running commentary of the first half of the race, using Donald's binoculars. Aside from a near-collision with a pair travelling in the opposite direction, the seat-racing proceeds to plan. Kip beats Dave Billings. Colin beats Dan. Pete beats Jake by a good 9 seconds, the extent of this margin a surprise to us all. Who would have thought that Pete's technical superiority would trounce Jake's power and aggression? Many of us, including myself, would have found it difficult to place bets on either, expecting the margin to be insignificant. But a win this convincing effectively means that our dentist has secured himself a seat in the Blue Boat – quite a contrast to last year's seat-racing when he wasn't fast enough even to make the spare pair. And not bad for someone who took up rowing only a few years ago after he'd broken his leg trialling at rugby for Derbyshire County.[19]

Standing on top of the umpire's tower, we hear him cry out across the deep, tranquil green waters – a genuine and primordial roar of victory over his adversary. For Pete it's finally over. His demon lies slain. He has atoned, at last, for that dismal showing a year ago today. Last summer's preparation for the new season, the tedious, painful 80-minute erg sessions, the lifting of weights, all of it pre-breakfast and ad nauseam; the many tank sessions, the scrutinising of long reams of footage of his own rowing as shot from the coaching launches – his numbers have finally come up. And by God does he know it.

Jake, by contrast, is inconsolable. The agonising pain and disappointment are easily visible, even from this distance. His head hangs drooping like a flower out of bloom, his spirit extinguished – everyone absorbed in the magnitude of the moment, the 'great weight of the unspoken' leaving them little to talk about. Should he not make the Blue Boat, a prospect which is now entirely plausible, even likely, his chances of making the US Olympic team are slim too, and he's well aware of this. After all, he was told in no uncertain terms by his US team coach that applying to Cambridge could be a mistake – that he would be much better off training full-time with the US squad. Going to Cambridge meant he'd be on his own without a support network back home. Thus, much is riding on Jake making the Blue Boat. Even Pete has gone quiet.

> So through that unripe day you bore your head,
> And the day was plucked and tasted bitter[20]

Bakes, Grant, Linda and I meanwhile stand by meditatively, taking in the scene from atop the hardwood tower.

Me: 'Looks like the end of the road for Jake—'

Grant: 'It does, doesn't it?'

Linda: 'Such a nice guy too.'

Bakes: 'True.'

Me: 'Good on Pete though, isn't it?'

Grant: 'It is.'

Linda: 'He's nice too.'

(Pause)

Bakes: 'I'm fuckin' starving …'

Chapter 19

It's New Year's Eve and a few minutes past nine. As agreed before showers, I meet some of the squad at reception for a gentle stroll to the rather ordinary lakeside bistro that will provide tonight's entertainment. From outside, the front parlour looks abandoned, its deserted bar lit up by a single fluorescent rod bolted to yellowed, crusty ceiling tiles. Movement behind the aluminium-framed glass entrance suggests the presence of life, however, and the proprietor, smiling broadly, directs us to a large function room through a set of double doors at the very back of the building. This having been designated an all-purpose room, it serves no purpose – at least none other than that of providing a place for people like us, away from home at a time of year when nothing's more desirable than to be at home, in an alien town with alien people and alien food, on the biggest night of the year but with no time to recover from hangovers, and so with no real plans to do anything memorable.

It smells funny too, like bleach and fried fish and plasterboard. The walls are austere and the few ornaments beastly. In one corner sits a white toy horse on a large metal spring. One of the walls features a gigantic jigsaw puzzle of a long-lost landscape, framed inside four unpainted strips of pine. Several of the pieces have been peeled off at some point, leaving ugly bald patches. The whole damn thing feels like a big fucking waiting room, a place to fritter away the odd few hours between the old and the new. There's the odd balloon announcing the festive season, and hip Spanish music alien to all oozing through ceiling-mounted speakers. The whole shebang is well intended but kitsch and nauseating and best forgotten.

With little or no food in our stomachs, the cheap Spanish wine hits the spot pretty quickly. Little plastic bags of green grapes, twelve in all, and designed to be eaten one at a time on every stroke of the clock at midnight, are torn open almost as soon as we've sat down.

The wine tonight is a rare treat in an environment ordinarily almost free of alcohol. But it's New Year's Eve after all, and tonight will give the boys a chance to let their hair down, to crack the shell and break out of this nerve-racking selection process, even if only for a few hours. However, having tee-totalled for the best part of three-and-a-half months, Russ is feeling the effect of the alcohol more quickly than anyone. His small coxswain frame and 57 kilograms leave him ill-prepared to compete with the 100kg-plus bulk of the oarsmen. I take a snap or two as he sits parked in a green plastic chair, a little tipsy, top button undone and nodding indecisively as he focuses on the spectacle in front of him. But with one eye having called it a day and the other twisted like Orwell's mongrel, this is becoming increasingly difficult.

With just two more minutes to go until the New Year, Russ slurs that he's heading out of hell and back to the hotel. He pushes back his chair and stands upright, or tries to, both eyes having now closed up shop. In this state he's unlikely to go anywhere soon, I think (foolishly as it happens).

'Come on, room-mate,' I try, 'only two more minutes until midnight ...'

I steady him with my arm wrapped tightly around his shoulder. Our friend the proprietor hurries into the room with an old tape recording of Big Ben striking twelve. I look at him bemused as he fiddles with the tape player in a race against the clock, putting the tape in wrong the first time, then, having examined the label, getting it in the right way round. Finally he beats time and gets the damn chiming started a full 30 seconds early. Other than me, nobody seems to notice or care and I swallow my protest and herald in the New Year noisily and also prematurely. Marco, the only oarsman authentically Spanish, having managed to hold on to his bag of twelve grapes, conscientiously chews one grape for every chime.

Shortly afterwards, the boys begin to take their leave. I look in vain for Russ, who has disappeared. When I arrive at the room some twenty minutes later, I find him fast asleep, lights turned on, sprawled out on top of the bed clothes. I get undressed, throw back the sheets, turn off the lights, and manage to get comfortable without raising the alarm.

All I remember next is being woken up by Russ stumbling noisily through the dark hotel room en route to the toilet. I flick on my reading light. Russ, caught unawares by its brilliance, keels over sideways and onto the half-inch crevice separating our two beds. Obligingly, our makeshift bed opens her legs to receive Russ head-first. And there he remains, dead to the world. I prod him.

But Russ seems resigned to the status quo. I wriggle my right hand underneath his side and follow the hollow of his back until it reappears, grab hold of his right elbow with my free hand, and bit by bit hoist him up. Russ, once back on his legs, shuffles into the bathroom for a pee. I let the crack between the beds be – grateful for the problem it helped solve – and sit on the bed waiting, sick for want of sleep. I am also ill at ease.

'Russ,' I say after things have gone quiet, 'you okay?'

Reluctantly I get up and hobble into the bathroom, not sure what to expect. Inside it, Russ is standing at an angle, his shoulder blades resting against the bathroom wall, his trousers still halfway down, and him fast asleep.

'Let's get you into bed so you can sleep it off.'

Russ throws his head back in what appears to be a concession that the current arrangement is unsustainable. He mutters something incoherent and allows me to support him by the waist back into the bedroom. A few minutes later, he's in bed once more, undressed this time, but insisting that he sleep underneath his mattress cover.

I pull a blanket over him, turn out the light, and descend into Gehenna, to face my own demons.

CHAPTER 20

New Year's Day, 2007

Day 1 of 365 is predictably ho-hum. Having correctly anticipated us feeling raw after last night's dinner, Duncan decides
to give us a day off, bar a run around the lake. It's a gorgeous
morning, refreshing and cool, but comfortable enough to venture
outside without a jacket. The only excitement is today's move from
Hotel l'Ast to Hotel Mirallac, a four-star abode right on the lake.
It has modern and comfortable rooms and, above all, wireless
internet access. No sooner has this discovery been announced than
we leg it over to the white marble hotel lobby, park ourselves on
the red cloth sofas or around coffee tables, laptop in hand, and log
on. Within ten minutes, fourteen of us are online. Donald walks
in, wearing his usual light blue Cambridge fleece, looking inquisitively at us tapping feverishly on our keyboards. He sits down
right opposite Colin and me, on an identical red sofa, and falls
asleep.

Russ, Marco and I share a double room (a collapsible camping
bed has been wheeled in for Marco). We spend the day relaxing in
and around the hotel: reading, checking Facebook profiles, doing
laundry, moving stuff from one hotel to the next, playing poker or
watching DVDs. The award-winning TV show *24* is a particular
favourite, and the guys have brought along two complete series –
48 continuous hours of watching, collectively poring over a
plasma laptop screen. It's seriously addictive stuff.

After their daily dose of *24*, most opt for an early night. Several
of them will be seat-raced tomorrow. With Pete Champion secure

in 3 seat, and Kip at bow, we must now find our 2 and 4 seats. If tomorrow is successful, Duncan may be able to announce a tentative Blue Boat line-up in two days' time.

Tuesday, 2 January

'Man, it's cold ...' whispers Russ. I too woke up several times during the night, shivering. Marco gets out of bed first, the backlight of his mobile phone illuminating a makeshift path between our strewn-about bags, clothes, cox-boxes, energy bars, battery rechargers, toiletries, laptops and books, until he finds the thermostat.

'No wonder,' he croaks, 'it's fifteen fucking degrees in here.' He turns up the dial and, almost immediately, a noisy fan coughs into motion somewhere in the dark above our heads. He walks into the bathroom, switches on the light, and pees noisily.

This morning's seat-racing is decisive in configuring a shadow Blue Boat. With four bow-siders and two stroke-siders now in place, today's battle will be between Dan, Don, Colin and Oli for the last two remaining seats. Donald, Rob, Linda and I head for the tower, stopwatches dangling from our necks, to keep track of finishing times. After five 1,500-metre races in two coxed fours, Dan and Oli remain within one second of each other. Don, alas, in a performance reminiscent of Jake's two days ago, has lost all races. This essentially rules him out of the Blue Boat yet again, having come so close twelve months ago too. With Colin now firmly in 2 seat, having convincingly won all his races, this leaves Duncan with the challenge of deciding between Oli and Dan for 4 seat. Oli began well with a strong performance on the erg early in the season, but fell ill and had a poor showing on his pre-Christmas 5k. Technically, however, he seems superior to Dan, particularly when it comes to rowing in that quintessentially Cambridge style. Dan has really come on well since the start of the season, has lost some weight and put down an excellent 5k result of 15:46. He is liked by the boys and generally seen to be a force for good in the boat.

When the coaches meet to discuss the results after lunch, it's clear that deciding between the two is far from straightforward. If the Boat Race were tomorrow, Oli's technical superiority would be more valuable than Dan's comparative physical strength and positive demeanour. However, Dan's physiology could be an asset in the longer term if he were able to shape up technically, primarily in lengthening his stroke to match that of the rest of the crew. Oli has rowed the Boat Race twice before in Goldie and his experience with the Tideway's potentially rough conditions is an asset. At the same time, Dan has rowed competitively from the age of thirteen, including as an international, so is the more experienced racer.

After a lengthy debate around the various possible alternative combinations, Duncan decides to put out something close to the Blue Boat, swapping Dan and Colin midway through the outing. With Thorsten at stroke, followed by Seb, Kieran, Tom, Oli, and Pete, and with Kip in bow seat, this will allow us to carefully observe Dan and Oli at work simultaneously, with Dan at 2 and Oli at 4, looked at carefully from the stern and side. As Oli seems a slight favourite, Colin will be swapped with Dan to possibly end up with the first-ever configuration of the 2007 Cambridge Blue Boat. All is set for a volatile afternoon.

Wednesday, 3 January

Yesterday produced its fair share of excitement, but also difficulties. Duncan, having called all the guys together at the waterfront, announced the crew line-ups. Dan and Oli were put in what all the athletes would have regarded as the shadow Blue Boat, with the intention, of course, to compare their technical performance, and, midway through the outing, to swap Dan for Colin. Colin seemed surprised at this, but then he doesn't know that he has pretty much secured a seat in the boat already, that he's been put with the Goldie boys merely as a short-term alternative to allow for a visual comparison of Oli and Dan rowing simultaneously. Or at least that's the plan.

After the afternoon outing, and as the sun descends gently on the lake, Duncan suggests we might have a brief meeting of the coaches to finalise selection for the provisional Blue Boat. Duncan explains that Oli's technique, though not perfect, is far more consistent with the Cambridge approach than Dan's, and that he will have a word with each of the affected athletes. None of the coaches raises objections, though, in all fairness, only Duncan and Grant were able to get a good visual of the shadow Blue Boat. The video footage they took is, unfortunately, not available for review as the camcorder's playback function has given up the ghost. A minor inconvenience at the time, or so it seemed, but one that will be partly responsible for what's to come.

Dan takes Duncan's decision badly – but not nearly as badly as do the five returning Blues. No sooner has Duncan sat back down in the hotel lobby than Tom and Seb come storming in, heading straight for our table, and demanding to have a word, in private, with Duncan. They are furious. Even Tom, normally among the most composed, sees red. Duncan pushes back his chair and stands up. I look over at Bakes, who shrugs his shoulders. Neither of us have any idea what this is about, except that it all seems deadly serious. Seb points in the direction of the hotel bar. The three of them leave the lobby through the glass doors and head into the bar. Bakes and I stay put, each with a book in hand but no longer any real desire to read.

When Duncan returns to our table, he looks distinctly uncomfortable. Seb and Tom, he says, are unhappy, disagreeing with our selection and dismayed that they weren't consulted on the decision. Surely, they'd have views on the matter? Views that matter? After all, coaches may be able to get a good visual impression of the boat but aren't necessarily a good judge of the 'feel' of the boat. Tom, by contrast, lacks this visual impression but as one of the crew, and as a conduit for the other athletes, is able to provide feedback on 'how it felt' as well as explain and defend Duncan's decision to the triallists.

It's unusual for rowers to demand this much input in crew selection. Ordinarily, coaches make final selection decisions and whether the rowers think them fair or judicious is neither here nor there. The reason, I suspect, that many top coaches have been able to get away with this is because they have so often proved correct in the past. This is true for Oxford's Sean Bowden, Canada's Mike Spracklen, and Great Britain's Jürgen Gröbler. With a long and impressive string of international medals or Boat Race wins, coaches' decisions may be neither popular nor even considered impartial or sensible, but are usually taken at face value. By contrast, Duncan has yet to win a Boat Race.

Establishing one's reputation as a world-class rowing coach is a tall order even in ordinary conditions. But this is no ordinary squad – with two reigning World Champions, one former Olympic gold medallist and World Champion, two world bronze medallists, and several others who have competed at international level, either as juniors or seniors, Duncan is faced with a dysfunctional group of strong, loosely-tied individuals. What makes these guys attractive makes them difficult too: they respect only their peers, they want to be the best and yet are contemptuous of those inferior to themselves, and they are extraordinarily strong-willed (which both fuelled and fuels their achievements). Given the circumstances, Duncan has little choice but to adopt democratic means of making selection decisions. If tonight's showing proves anything, it's that they are to be ignored only at his peril. Not an enviable position to be in.

Leaving aside the question of their not being consulted on the decision, the five returning Blues think it a terrible mistake not to have included Dan O'Shaughnessy in the provisional Blue Boat line-up. His personality seems to make a surprisingly positive difference to their sense of 'togetherness'. Dan reminds the two German internationals of a similarly positive experience earlier in the year, when their Deutschlandachter benefited from having one oarsman in the boat who was not outstanding technically but was able somehow to make the crew gel – providing that crucial slab of adhesive that kept the guys together as a team. Dan's personality, likewise, made a difference to the Fairbairns and Trial Eights crews, and with neither Oli nor Colin being particularly talkative, Dan might help breathe life into the bow section of the boat. As Tom explains, a fast boat is judged not by the stern four (who will usually be the strongest rowers anyway) but by its bow four. And that's where Dan may come in handy.

Thursday, 4 January

At Tom's request the coaches and returning Blues meet at 1:30pm in the hotel bar. The agenda is obvious. After yesterday's events, Tom wants to have a look at the seat-racing results himself, even if they confirm what Duncan already told him: that Colin was faster than Don by 8 seconds, that Colin beat Dan by a small margin, and that Dan and Oli are about on a par with each other. This information should be helpful, if only to confirm that if Dan were to be put in the Blue Boat, it would be in exchange for Oli rather than Colin. Thus far, the request has been that of swapping Dan for Colin. Whether this suggests a strong preference for Dan or a far more innocent misconception that Dan beat Colin in seat-racing (rather than the other way around) is unclear at this stage. Duncan, with the support of Bakes and Donald, explains the rationale for yesterday's selection decision in some detail while also acknowledging that not having consulted Tom was a mistake. Tom, in reply, suggests that a meeting of minds might help clear the air gathering around the table – not just for us but for the other four returning Blues. The guys worry about what they see as favouritism in selection and a deliberate attempt to keep information limited and justifications obscure. Tom wonders: would I please facilitate this meeting?

'Not a problem,' I say, far more confidently than warranted by my limited experience, and wander off to find us a meeting room for tomorrow afternoon. I can already feel the adrenaline surging inside – a mixture of dread and excitement (but mostly dread).

Duncan is visibly hurt by what he sees as accusations of cronyism. Being accused of making mistakes or of being insensitive is unpleasant but fair enough. But to be accused of nepotism is to question that very core of his personhood, his integrity. It's a distinctly alienating experience, and one he's seen before many a time, he says.

Dinner that evening is dreadful. The food is fine but the atmosphere tense. The air is thick with misgiving. The possibility of a revolution weighs heavily on the minds of Duncan and the five returning Blues. The last thing anyone wants is a repeat of the Oxford mutiny of 1987. Tonight's seating arrangement is telling. A handful of athletes have wandered off to an Italian restaurant for pizza. Those that haven't sit grouped together at separate tables well away from the coaches. The usual chatter has been reduced to a whispering campaign. There is a clear disconnection, for the first time this season, between coaches and athletes – capital and labour – a division marked by distrust and hostility.

After dessert, the guys return to watching 24, an episode whose plotline mirrors the chilling distrust between the squad and coaches here tonight. We stare at the plasma self-consciously. Silently.

AUDREY RAINS: Well, what can we do about it?
BILL BUCHANAN: Nothing. Gill is in charge.
AUDREY RAINS: He may be in charge, but he's not in control.*

*From the TV show 24, series 5, episode 3:00pm–4:00pm.

CHAPTER 21

Friday, 5 January

We assemble around a long, veneered wooden table in a dark-ish, nauseatingly warm reception room. Were it not for the furry carpeted floor, it might have doubled as a ballroom. I pull back the heavy curtains. The rays of the sun capture the zillions of dust particles lazily floating about, in no hurry to settle down and happily inhaled. Tom props open the door to let some coolness in. The outside air wastes no time in attacking the stuffiness inside.

Kip has opted for a seat at the far end of the mahogany table, his head cupped in his left hand, elbow on the table. Kieran sits opposite, his posture the exact mirror image of Kip's. Next to Kieran and closer to me are Thorsten, Bakes and Duncan, in that order, balanced out by Seb and Tom on the other side. I sit at the far corner, one table leg lodged uncomfortably between my knees. My approach today is a replica of that used with the 'troubled four' several weeks ago.

'Before we start, we'll need to agree on some ground rules,' I begin, somewhat hot under the collar. Seven pairs of eyes stare back apprehensively, each a minute window into the soul that lies beyond. 'What happens here stays here. Whatever we do here we don't talk about outside of the walls of this room.' The point, of course, being to create an environment in which each will feel free to speak his mind with no fear of it coming to haunt him later on.

'Second, we stay in this room until we've resolved this thing, or at least have come as close to resolving it as we can. There's no throwing toys out of the pram and no huffing and puffing and leaving the room in anger. We stay put until we've talked this through ...'

'Third, when one of you talks, everyone else listens. There will be a chance for you to respond in due course.'

'And fourth, you need to understand that there is no silver bullet. There is no guarantee that this process will lead to a good outcome for all. But at least we can give it a shot, seeing where we're now stranded –'

(Silence.)

'... Happy to agree to these ground rules?'

They nod. Seb grunts. Of course they do, they wouldn't have turned up otherwise. Besides, the rules are perfectly reasonable, and how can one refuse to be reasonable? But by agreeing to these rules they'll have committed to listening to each other and to airing their own views and concerns freely – which is no small step forward from the present stalemate. Encouraged, I outline the structure of what is really a conventional mediation process. There are four parts to it, I explain. First, going around the table, we will all say what we think would be a good outcome of this meeting. 'Walking out of the room in two hours' time, what is it you would like to have achieved?' This startlingly straightforward question accomplishes two things: it commits those present to a clear vision of their objective and it allows them to understand the objectives of others too. What will surprise them (as it did that humid afternoon) is that the desired outcomes of all those present are virtually identical. Knowing that we all want pretty much the same thing makes solving problems that much more straightforward.

'Second, tell us how you feel about the problem. Don't worry yet about what you think the problem is, but tell us how it makes you feel.' What I'm attempting here is to try to pry the problem from its highly emotive context by allowing the athletes to spill their guts with one crucial difference: by virtue of our rules, they know that this time, for once, they are listened to. And what an unbelievable difference that makes.

'Third, let's take a look at the actual problem.' Often, the problem, once detached from its emotional baggage, is reasonably straightforward to resolve. This afternoon, the returning Blues want reassurance that Blue Boat selection is not final, that there is more trialling to be had – even during this camp – and that Dan will be given a fair chance to make the crew. Their strong defence of Dan is interesting. They appear less concerned with Dan's technical prowess than with his ability to gel the boat socially. His gusto, cheerfulness and confidence may not translate into better boat-moving ability on an individual level, but they seem to get a better performance out of the other seven oarsmen. By helping them to gel into a single rhythm, he adds considerably to boat speed. I admit to being surprised (though perhaps I shouldn't have been) that even in such a technically demanding sport as rowing, sociability can trump skilfulness – not just because Dan lightens the mood, but because he helps them dig deeper inside themselves. What if he really is that missing ingredient?

Finally, once the problem has been identified and dealt with in a rational manner, each oarsman and coach commits to a 'take-away' promise. These typically take the form of: 'Next time I will do such-and-such. At the same time, I cannot do this by myself and I need you to do that-and-the-other ...' It may sound corny, but it seems to work. It allows everyone not just to accept shared responsibility for the problem and its solution but to call upon someone else in articulating what it is they commit to doing themselves. The solution, in other words, begins with one's own contribution but doesn't end there. None of it is rocket-science really, but then hardly anything genuinely useful in life ever is.

Though not without its poignant moments, the hour-and-a-half is well spent. Duncan is reaffirmed as top dog, Bakes is content that even oarsmen as experienced as they are will take coaching advice on board, Tom seems satisfied that the dust has settled, and the rest are secure in the knowledge that their opinions will be taken into account when making selection decisions. All in all, not a bad day at the office, as Duncan puts it.

He looks exhausted.

❖

After a trip out to the medieval city of Besalu, 10 kilometres from Banyoles, we return in time for the evening's entertainment: an impromptu cinematic treat. Seb and Thorsten, having just returned from a shopping spree, flaunt their bounty: a 24-can pack of Hefeweissbier. The lukewarm wheat-based lager goes down nicely, and in stark contrast to yesterday, the atmosphere is upbeat. We watch one of the Rocky movies, starring a pumped-up, inarticulate Sylvester Stallone. Donald, sitting at the very back of our improvised theatre, provides the usual commentary, quite clueless as to what the film is about but amusing and oddly comforting nonetheless.

I sit back contentedly and enjoy the ambience of camaraderie renewed.

CHAPTER 22

Over lunch today, Dan is once more the focal point of the coaches' discussion. Is he *really* a catalyst, able to help the rest of the crew raise their game? If so, what does this mean for the relevance of conventional methods of crew selection, things like erg tests, pair matrices, seat-racing? Is there an objective, foolproof way of measuring the contributions of triallists to the performance of the crew as a unit? How can one measure what difference the swapping of one oarsman with another makes to the relative contributions of all the other rowers with any degree of precision? After all, in traditional seat-racing, the rest of the crew could, even subconsciously, rig the trials by rowing just that little bit suboptimally to prevent certain individuals from making the cut. And how does one navigate a situation where senior oarsmen are willing to disregard objective trial results so as to get their man in the boat? And how does one treat seat-racing results that are inconsistent? These are tough questions to answer – and even tougher selection criteria to defend.

Sunday, 7 January

Jake decided to leave camp early. His engineering course requires him to attend a week of pre-term lectures. Given the circumstances, it's probably not a bad idea for Jake to head back to Cambridge, allowing him to mull over his dismal showing in private. Duncan's asked me to drive him to the airport, a trip that ordinarily wouldn't take more than 25 minutes or so. Jake's terribly subdued, his self-confidence at an all-time low. His poor showing at seat-racing was a real kick in the teeth, having pulled such strong numbers on the erg and after four very successful years of rowing at Stanford. We listen to Johnny Cash pluck at his guitar as we snake our way out of Banyoles' historic centre and onto the asphalt en route to the airport.

'Any thoughts on this past week?' I venture carefully.

'I guess I'm not sure that I've got what it takes. I just don't get what they want me to do. I pull my guts out and I'm still not movin' the boat.'

'You've got potential. No one's ever questioned that.'

'Maybe …'

'It's really just a matter of technique.'

'But that's the frustrating thing … If only it were a matter of physiology, I'd know what to do, but with technique, it's all like—'

'A dark art?'

'Sort of …'

Jake had looked forward to the seat-racing, certain that he'd be able to confirm what most already expected: that he would definitely make the Blue Boat. After all, he hadn't lost a single seat-race while rowing at Stanford. He's always loved seat-racing, probably because he's good at it; it allows him to put his footprint firmly on the map as someone to take seriously. Losing every single race in Banyoles proved confusing and unsettling to his self-identity. He'd always thought of himself as first and foremost an elite sportsman, a world-class rower, and now that final bastion risks imploding.

We're on the motorway now and the straightforward driving gives us plenty of time to talk. Jake embarks on a monologue.

'What the fuck is going on? If I'm not a good rower then what am I? Lost every fucking race in every single boat. That's horrible, to be the guy that when people see you in their boat they think they're gonna lose—'

I avoid eye contact, my gaze focused on the black canvas ahead and below.

'Having been on the other side I know how people talk. You

just know when they see stuff like this what they say, and that's really isolating. You feel so alone ... and then along with that is the idea of having to explain what happened to everyone back home who really wanted me to do well. That fucking sucks—'

Jake's sense of self has always been inextricably bound up with his rowing. With this falling to bits, everything else vanishes too. As I look at Jake sideways, I see none of the self-confident, good-humoured athlete of a few days ago. As in Dante's *Divine Comedy*: not dead and yet nothing of life remains. No longer a man but the shell of one.

Jake sees life for what it is – an ongoing negotiation between the purposeful and void, between the desire for independence and the realisation that one is destined to be interdependent, caught between contentment and despair, wanting to live and wishing to die; or if not to die then simply, at the flick of a finger, not to be.

'It really feels that bad sometimes.'

To want to go as did Roth's Everyman, being 'no more, freed from being, entering into nowhere without even knowing it'; it's here that life is most precarious: being tempted to switch off the lights and call it a day.

> How did I get into the world? Why was I not asked about it and why was I not informed of the rules and regulations but just thrust into the ranks as if I had been bought by a peddling shanghaier of human beings? How did I get involved in this big enterprise called actuality? Why should I be involved? Isn't it a matter of choice? And if I am compelled to be involved, where is the manager – I have something to say about this. Is there no manager? To whom shall I make my complaint?[21]

So what is it that prevents Jake from throwing in the towel? Is it that he fears, with Rushdie's midnight child, absurdity? Of having lived a pointless life pointlessly? Is Jake's life any less absurd than that of such fictional personas as Camus's Meursault or Celine's Bardamu?

'Look on the bright side,' I suggest. 'To improve technically need not be a gradual process. For Wanne and Oli things suddenly just fell into place; the stuff they'd worked on for so long, when one day things are explained in a slightly different way and suddenly click.'

'Maybe. But I feel like I've now got to decide whether I have what it takes to make the US Olympic squad or whether I should give up rowing altogether.'

'Would the American coach be okay if you just made Goldie?'

'I'm not sure – that's what I've got to find out.'

Me resorting to platitudes: 'Isn't it better to live with failure than regret?'

(No response.)

I drop a dispirited Jake off at the airport terminal. How different Jake's state of mind was when arriving here a week ago, full of energy and with a clear shot at the Blue Boat.

The evening coaches' meeting is tough. As usual, we gather in the smoke-filled bar next door to the hotel. Unlike previous days, however, the bar is filled with noisy locals, forcing us to up the volume, and, with no scope for subtlety, haemorrhaging the conversation.

The Dan–Colin–Oli affair yet again dominates. Dan is still favoured by the five returning Blues. Oli is less impressive than Colin on the erg but looks like a better fit. Also, Kieran, Tom, Oli and Pete seem pretty exciting as a potential unit in the middle four seats of the boat. Earlier this week, they rowed the socks off any of the other crews in a coxless four and, even in the eight, look extremely good as a foursome. Colin, on the other hand, is more powerful. If the crew succeed in their bid for Dan, should Oli or Colin be left out? And what would the consequences of either option be? If Colin were to be left out, these might be significant. For one, the selection process would emerge as far more ambiguous, and subject to nepotism, than would be good for the club's future, giving more credence to subjective impressions and politicking than to objective test results. When athletes lose faith in selection processes as methodological and fair, they may try to improve their prospects by means of lobbying. If, on the other hand, Oli were to be relegated to the reserve boat, chances are that some of the senior oarsmen would be unhappy, as he not only looks like a better fit but, according to the crew, feels better than Colin does. But then, Colin pulls far better numbers. So, one faces the prospect of either telling Colin he's out and muddling up the selection process, or telling Oli he's out but without a good justification – for if Oli fails on the basis of test results, he shouldn't have been given a seat in the provisional Blue Boat in the first place. If he's told that, having compared him with Colin and Dan over the last few days, he doesn't fit, that would fly in the face of both what coaches have observed and athletes have felt. It seems Duncan is caught between a rock and a hard place, and not for the first time this season.

It's all getting a bit much for Tom, wedged between Donald and Bakes.

'I need some time to think – back in ten minutes.' Tom gets up and leaves the hotel bar.

Donald (mumbling): 'Not sure what that's all about—'

Duncan: 'He said he needs some time to think.'

And so there we sit, unable to carry on our discussion, and yet with nothing much else to talk about. Bakes starts fiddling around with his handset. Donald folds his hands across his considerable belly, sighs deeply, heavy eyelids half-shut, eyes cast on the table in front. Duncan coughs uncomfortably: 'Another beer anyone?'

Bakes: 'Yup.'

Me: 'I could use one.'

Donald: 'Still working on my first.'

Once Tom has re-entered the bar, the conversation picks up momentum.

'Okay,' Tom begins, 'what would make the fastest possible boat twelve weeks from now?'

Donald: 'I think Dan looks okay and that Oli looks better in 4 seat than Colin, frankly.'

Bakes: 'I agree with Dan fitting well in the boat but my personal preference would be for Colin. He's got the numbers.'

Tom: 'Duncan?'

Duncan: 'Do you think you can win the Boat Race with any of these nine guys?'

Tom: 'Yes I do actually—'

Duncan: 'Okay, well why not continue looking at the guys a little longer before we firm up the eight?'

Tom: 'True ...'

Duncan: 'Happy with that?'

Tom: 'Yes.'

Duncan: 'Okay. Go and get some sleep – you look like shit.'

CHAPTER 23

Monday, 8 January

The decisive selection meeting takes place on the penultimate day of camp. Duncan calls his coaching team into the hotel bar.

'What did you all make of Dan, Oli and Colin this morning?' Duncan gets straight to the point.

'Oli and Colin looked bloody awful, I thought.'

'Agree—'

'Far from ideal ...'

And that more or less settles it. Dan is in. An impressive feat for someone without any significant achievements this season bar one strong pre-Christmas 5,000-metre erg test. The decision over the last remaining seat (4 seat) swings in Oli's favour, principally because he seems to provide a better overall fit with the rest of the crew. Russ will cox the Blue Boat.

'That's the line-up, then,' Duncan sighs. Everyone seems relieved that a decision has finally been made, allowing the crews to settle in, relax, and get on with the job of preparing for 7 April. Just one thing remains to be done: to prepare Colin, Rebecca, Marco, Richard Stutt and David Hopper for what's about to hit them.

Rebecca takes the news very badly. I find her walking towards the lake, her eyes puffy and bloodshot. She's a promising coxswain but her opposition just proved too strong. Russ has successfully steered two successive Goldie crews to victory on the Championship course. Hopper, Stutt and Marco are told that they'll be the designated reserves. Should any of the crew fall ill (which has happened often enough in the past to instil a glimmer of hope that they might make one of the boats after all), they will get a shot at Goldie. Colin, who secured a seat in the provisional Blue Boat earlier this week, is taken aside by Duncan and Bakes – the former to break the news, the latter to pick up the pieces. He's told that what he thought was a sure seat in the Blue Boat is no longer his. Instead, the last two provisional seats go to Dan, who is technically less close to the Cambridge ideal than Colin, and to Oli, who is physiologically weaker than both. Had they beaten him on both technique and numbers, the choice would have been obvious. How on earth is he going to deal with this, I think, and watch them in conversation some 40 yards from where I stand, Colin taking it on the chin like an Englishman.

When he reappears, his face betrays the anguish inside. His eyes are strained, his skin pale and drawn, his hands trembling involuntarily, his mind fogged up with bewilderment. Having won his seat-race, having registered impressive numbers on the erg tests, having bloody well met all objective criteria, how is he to satisfy those that are subjective? Those that depend on visual impressions from the coaching launches? On their intuition and gut feeling? On similarities drawn with past Boat Race crews, sometimes in the very distant past? In fact, it's quite striking to see the extent to which coaches rely on subjective judgements in making decisions. These judgements don't usually override objective assessments of performance, but they help coaches to differentiate between oarsmen who are on paper virtually identical; or if not identical, very close; or if not close, then prone to generating results that confuse. Such happens when you beat another oarsman in seat-racing who himself has just beaten someone who now beats you.

Selection, of course, is never based on a single criterion but instead relies on a combination of hard and soft data, on erg scores and visuals, on seat-racing and gut-feel, on current performance and memories of past performance. To paraphrase *Financial*

Times columnist John Kay, the attractiveness of a face, the happiness of a society, the progress of a civilisation, the potential of a rowing crew, is multi-dimensional: components of attractiveness, happiness, progress or potential are determined by subjective consensus and are not always susceptible to objective measurement. It is thus somewhat surprising, he says, that scientists and wannabe scientists such as economists resist the use of soft data. He quotes Lord Kelvin as having suggested that unless you can measure something, your knowledge is of a meagre kind. But of course, Kelvin also suggested that manned flight was impossible. Complex activities, like sweep rowing, can only be described with words, says Kay, using a combination of hard and soft data – hard data being supplements, not substitutes, for the evidence provided by eyes, guts and ears.

Duncan and Bakes, meanwhile, have rejoined the squad, facing the lake and the snowcapped mountains beyond. Twenty-two pairs of eyes stare back in reply. 'Provisional crews have been selected,' Duncan begins, 'and will remain in place for the time being. Before I tell you who's in which crew I want you to understand that no seat is ever guaranteed. All of you will continue to be carefully watched by us, both on the water and on the erg. Should anyone raise his game – or hers (and here he looks at Rebecca) – the coaches will evaluate this progress in light of the performance of everyone else and, based on this, decide whether a new seat-race is called for.' Here he looks up at his squad, most of whom will already have a fairly good idea as to who's in what boat, and would rather get the matter over with. For others, like Pete and Dan, it's their moment in the limelight.

Duncan stands fiddling with a folded piece of paper. On it are the names of those with a shot at a Cambridge Blue: Thorsten, Seb, Kieran, Tom, Oli, Pete, Dan and Kip, who will be coxed by Russ. The remainder of the squad will make up Goldie and the spare pair.

Tuesday, 9 January

First day for the provisional Blue and Goldie crews to be raced. Bristol University's first and second eight (who arrived on the lake a week ago for their own winter training camp) are awaiting our arrival on the deep green water. After a quick breakfast of cereal and sweet buns, we pack up and leave for the boatshed.

The Blue Boat crew assemble for core exercises and a pre-race chat. This being their first race together, the atmosphere is properly electric. The guys are on edge but positively so. This is their first opportunity to prove themselves as a crew, to each other and to the coaches – their chance to show the latter's scepticism to be without foundation.

Bristol is already on the water, warming up over the 2,000-metre stretch. Russ calls for 'The Flying Welshman' to be carried out of the boathouse (the boat to be used on Boat Race day has been left behind in Ely) and onto the lake. One by one they slide their oars across the light yellow shell and into the water, locking them securely against the black plastic buttons at the far end of the riggers. Placing one foot in the shell, they push off in unison. As the boat glides sideways into the lake, the athletes sit down to fasten the Velcro straps of their shoes, all the while holding on to their oar. After a 3,000-metre warm-up paddle, Goldie and the Blue Boat line up next to Bristol's two eights. Bristol will get a fifteen-second head start. Duncan will call the race.

'Bristol, ready? Attention. Go!', and Bristol is off. Cambridge follows shortly after, both eights drawing through the first three strokes, winding through the next five, and lengthening over another five. The Blue Boat gains a length on Goldie and on Bristol's second boat within the first 750 metres of the 2,000-metre course, and is rapidly catching up on Bristol's first. With only half the course to go they are overlapping. Bristol responds to Cambridge's aggression with a mighty push for twenty strokes. They are able to hold off our Blue Boat for a good 500 metres but in the last 300 they lose the plot. Russ calls for a higher rating over the last 250 metres. The crew respond immediately and, with 150 metres to go until the finish line, they row through Bristol, looking like a picture postcard – strong, relentless and, above all, *together*.

'Yesterday they looked like a crew set to lose the Boat Race,' mumbles Donald, 'yet now it looks like they might actually win it.' But of course the crew know the ball is now squarely in their court – that they were right and the coaches wrong. Dan O'Shaughnessy is their *cause*, the one thing the oarsmen collectively care about and have taken responsibility for; the one who seems to supply that key ingredient that cements them into a crew as opposed to a band of eight outrageously talented but conjointly dysfunctional individuals. What a note on which to conclude the training camp.

CHAPTER 24

'After Banyoles my goals changed quite drastically ...' Jake slurps audibly from a Paddington Bear mug of coffee, freshly brewed. We are sitting in my living room, he on a yellow sofa, me in a green chair, our feet separated by 50 inches of pine floorboard. It's been over a week since we returned from Spain, and the dust appears to have settled. Jake, like everyone, is back in training – and more determined than ever.

'They went from winning the Boat Race to being in the Boat Race. All I wanted was to make the Blue Boat and so all I did from then on was targeted squarely at that first-order goal and I knew I couldn't afford to mess up, to waste time – not any more – no room for error. From this point on it was the Blue Boat or nothing – pretty stark but that's really what it boiled down to: either I made the crew or I'd throw that and my Olympic dreams out of the window – and of course this had all sorts of consequences: for one I had to take myself far more seriously in relation to the other guys. From now on, if Dan or any of the others fell ill, that meant an opportunity for me because I got to replace him and had to make sure to make that session count, as I really could no longer afford to take things lightly – and this session, even if only a single session with the Blue Boat, could make all the difference to my future because it could show Duncan and Donald that I had a lot to offer. And so every session I had to be on my toes and make sure that it brought me closer to my objective, and I would listen to the coaches and made sure they'd got some video footage – and I would spend hours analysing the footage afterwards, and call

Duncan or Donald or Bakes to come in and watch the footage with me so I'd get a sense of what they wanted me to do, because it's easier for me to improve when I can see what good rowing is supposed to look like on video. I can't feel the difference between good rowing and Cambridge rowing – it's just rowing to me – you see, in the past when things go bad, like at Stanford, I just work harder at it no matter how much it hurts, because losing always hurts more. So I spent more time on the erg and next time pulled harder on the water – and so even that night in Banyoles the one thing that went through my mind was to make sure that I'd never feel like this ever again – it was horrible – I would wake up for days afterwards cheerfully and then suddenly remember what had happened and feel really miserable and then your heart just drops – it's a feeling that becomes more and more a part of you so that one day you wake up and you no longer feel cheerful but just feel shitty – and you just know that you don't want to feel that way ever again – you can't enjoy time with your friends, you can't talk to your mum on the phone, you find it difficult to talk, to laugh, to smile – I couldn't look the checkout lady at Tesco in the eye – couldn't look anyone in the eye – couldn't stand the sight of myself in the mirror. Melodramatic I know, but it was the most acute shame I have ever felt, like I betrayed myself and couldn't trust myself any more—'

As Jake carries on an uninterrupted monologue, it dawns on me as never before what a terrible blow the Banyoles seat-racing experience must have been to his sense of self, hinging so much on being top dog in the rowing community. No matter his stellar academic performance at Stanford, it's the rowing that really counts. It's this that comprises the raw material of his identity – that survival sense of who he is and forever wants to be.

'Having lost my seat-race was like finding out something about myself – something I didn't like seeing – I felt guilty – I felt guilty because I'd let my team-mates down, my friends, it's this incredible feeling of loss. If I do poorly in anything else it doesn't really matter, but if I do poorly in rowing that takes priority – because rowing matters in the way other things do not – and so the first thing I had to do when coming back from Banyoles was to learn to believe in myself again, and that was a very conscious effort. So I left early, which was good in retrospect as it gave me a couple of days to think and train on my own and allowed me to think about what it is I really wanted – and I really did think about quitting because it's fucking painful to look at yourself as having lost against everyone that matters. And so I had this fantasy of leaving camp and not telling anyone and bumming around Spain like a freak for a while – but that would have been running away from the problem, and I knew I didn't want that one seat-racing experience to be the thing to put me out of rowing – because like everyone I wanted to end my rowing career on a high note, and then I saw myself leaving Cambridge for the States to train there and salvage my chances of making the Olympic team – the method of training in Cambridge just felt too unnatural and I thought maybe if I got back into a programme that was more familiar then I would perform better too—'

Jake takes another sip of his coffee.

'And you know what, one of the worst thoughts is that once you know what you need to do to get back on track to make the Blue Boat, it would be incredibly tough mentally as well as physically – mentally because it meant I had to ask myself all sorts of questions like "Can I really do this?" and "How good am I really?" and "What am I worth?" – and did I really want the answers to these questions? What if I were to discover that I wasn't good enough, is that something I could live with? And it's so much harder to show everything you've got and put all your cards on the table than to say fuck this, and I don't really care – but then you have to admit to yourself that you do care, that you care very much, and that's probably the biggest hurdle. And then on the physical side the issues were mostly technical and it's not always clear whether I'm actually improving – because it's like when I used to go swimming in a lake near our house in the summer, and the lake had an island in the middle of it, and my brother and I used to go out and swim to the island, and whenever I would pop up my head out of the water to look how far the island was, it still seemed as far as before – and so these technical changes were scary but I knew that if I kept working, the changes would come along – just like how I always knew that if I kept swimming in the right direction I would make it to the island – all you can do is to keep your head down and push, and keep pushing, but I had no idea of what I needed to do to get to where I needed to be. I knew what it took to make the Stanford boat feel good but have no idea what I need to do to make this boat feel good, and the coaches here use many of the same words they did at Stanford but they seem to mean different things here and so it's pretty confusing and I often don't know what on earth they want me to do. And then seeing the guys again after Banyoles was really tough – particularly when you know that everyone talks about you behind your back and everyone's watching to see how you will respond – and you know people are saying things about you – and I felt a lot of animosity towards the guys and to Duncan in particular because it's hard to try and believe in yourself if no one else is believing in you. I knew I had given them every reason to think that I couldn't do it, but it fills you with anger to look around at each of your team-mates and think you probably don't think I can do it ... and you don't think I can do it either ... and you don't think I can do it – and even though they were all making a rational call based on the evidence, the only way I could respond was by saying fuck you, you don't know me – and I was also angry because I felt Duncan and Bakes should have spotted my technical faults earlier and helped me to avoid all this bullshit – I was so embarrassed – and so I made myself a recording—'

At that I sit up. 'What recording?'

'Just something I'd listen to all day long every day – cooking breakfast – before training – walking to class – brushing my teeth – studying – shopping for food – washing dishes – during training – after training – to try and get me to believe in myself again. Believing in yourself is the hardest part, because to do that you have to reject everything else that coaches and team-mates and results are telling you to believe—'

Listening to Jake's tape is a sobering experience, and one that provides a rare glimpse into the haunted soul of a 22-year-old struggling to restore confidence in himself. It may also bring us closer to what it is that differentiates these mortals from most: the ability and resourcefulness to climb back out of the cesspool of failure, to be hit hard and yet get back to their feet to face the one devil they'd much prefer to avoid: themselves. It's the courage to begin rebuilding brick by brick what the storms took down – knowing full well that there's no guarantee of success – that those on the outside may at long last be vindicated in their ridicule.

Nobody can work like I can
I have seen things they've not seen, and done things they've not done, and that makes me stronger
I beat Cal and Washington, because I worked for four years
I will beat Colin and Oli, because I will work for the next four weeks
There is no perfect job, there is no perfect house, there is no perfect wife
You work and then you die

I dominate the port side
I'm faster than Oli
I'm faster than Colin
I row faster than them, and I need to make Duncan and my team-mates see that I'm faster
I'm stronger than them
I work harder than them
I catch quicker, I pull harder, I move boats better than they do
Everyone wants me in 4 seat because I'm the fastest and the strongest
I learn every training session because every training session is an opportunity to get what I want

My catches are the quickest on the team

My catches are the quickest on the team
I get my fucking blade in the water faster than anybody else
I grip the water early and hang through my shoulders to move the boat
I'm the strongest rower alive
I win because I work the hardest
I get better every day and I learn faster than anybody else

I sit in the 4 seat of the Blue Boat because I adapt to everyone else and make them move faster
Everyone wants me in 4 seat because they know I am the best for the job
My catch is the quickest on the team

I am ruthless in my preparation
I work harder than anybody else
I get better faster than anybody else
I enjoy the pain and satisfaction of pushing myself to the limit
I am a tough, determined and persistent competitor who refuses to give in, no matter how difficult the situation may seem
I am calm and composed under pressure and totally committed to making the Blue Boat

I make boats move fast
I know that I'm preparing every day for the moment I can claim my seat, and I know that I will be ready when it comes
I make boats move fast
I sit in 4 seat of the Blue Boat

I will start at the bottom and work my way up
I am descended from the few that worked the hardest and fought their way to the top
No family has fought like mine has

Nobody can work like I can
I am sitting in 4 seat of the Blue Boat

'And so I decided to focus on showing Duncan and the Blue Boat how good I could be. The way I viewed it, it wasn't really a matter of who was the better oarsman between Colin, Oli and me – all that mattered was who was perceived to be better – and so I spent a lot of time thinking of how others would perceive me and I became overly sensitive to how I thought people saw me – particularly Duncan and Bakes – of how they thought I compared to Colin and Oli, and I sort of knew it helped that I was taller than either of them and I looked more like the natural oarsman – and I particularly wanted the coaches to see me working hard because if you're the guy when they walk into the boathouse and see you working, it gives them the impression that you work continuously. And so I also desperately wanted the guys in the Blue Boat to see that I was working hard, but at the same time I didn't want Colin and Oli to see me working hard because then they might start working hard too – and I didn't want them to find out until it was too late – and so they wouldn't feel threatened until it was time to threaten them on the river, though I did feel badly about this because I like Colin and Oli and feel sad about having to compete with them for a place in the Blue Boat, Oli especially as we were really good friends at the beginning of the season, whereas now it's tough to act normal around him when I've spent so much time targeting him as the guy I have to beat – a shame really, but what do you say to the people you are training yourself to hate? I wish I could train without cultivating such negative thoughts, but anger is the only thing that works for me and so this was the way it had to be. The fact that they were my friends meant that I knew things about them that could be perceived as insecurities that could work to my advantage, but I really didn't want to exploit them – I mean even in my own thoughts – but the mind games that I played with myself were so intense and I wanted so badly to get inside their heads and let them know I was the alpha male – it's so confusing to mentally attack your friends – it drives you insane but sanity seemed like a small price to pay for something I wanted so badly.'

(What Jake hadn't realised was that Colin too had been spending extra time on the ergometer, working hard at improving his technique, but out of view of the coaches and squad.)

Jake was born the first of four children in the small American town of Magnolia, Arkansas, in many ways a temporary reprieve from upstate New York, from where the family originally hailed and to which they would shortly return. The cultural differences between the liberal North and Baptist South made life complicated for Jake's free-spirited parents. Having moved back to New York state, the family rented a duplex in a town called Brooktondale – they living on the ground floor and another family on top of them. When ultimately this situation too proved unsustainable, his father built them a house on a nearby vacant lot – a simple home with two storeys, tan-coloured wooden sidings and red-painted shutters. To make space for his two younger siblings, Jake voluntarily moved to the basement, a permanently unfinished room with uncovered cinder-black walls and a concrete, uncarpeted floor. The occasional mouse, frog or snake would creep in, and whenever it rained, the basement would flood. To try at least to create a pretence of comfort, Jake hung sheets from the ceiling to simulate walls and collected carpet scraps from a local store to cover the concrete floor. In this environment he began his physical training, fashioning a boxing bag out of a pillowcase stuffed with sand, doing pull-ups from the girders, and hanging buckets of paint from the end of a hockey stick as a primitive but effective form of bench press.

'I loved it. While other kids were being told not to write on their walls, I could build and rebuild my room into whatever I wanted. I was in control.

'When Biff my brother and I were old enough, my dad sent us to play ice hockey in a local league – practices beginning at five o'clock on January mornings sent some of our team-mates off the ice crying from fingers and toes frozen by temperatures below minus 20 degrees centigrade. Biff and I both played goalie – tough stuff mentally and emotionally because we would beat ourselves up over every single goal we let through – we were hard on ourselves and ended up having a pretty tough time sometimes – the cold didn't help and the whole thing sucked – and then our dad decided to make us memorise a poem, of all things—

The longer I live, the more I realise the impact of attitude on life.

Attitude, to me, is more important than facts.

It is more important than the past, than education, than money, than circumstances, than failures, than successes, than what other people think or say or do.

It is more important than appearance, giftedness or skill. It will make or break a company – a church – a home.

The remarkable thing is we have a choice every day regarding the attitude we will embrace for that day.

We cannot change our past – we cannot change the fact that people will act in a certain way.

We cannot change the inevitable.

The only thing we can do is play on the one string we have, and that is our attitude – I am convinced that life is 10 per cent what happens to me and 90 per cent how I react to it.

And so it is with you—

We are in charge of our attitudes.[22]

'My dad wouldn't let us do anything else until we'd memorised this poem – we had to memorise the damn poem—'

Jake's rowing career began at the age of fifteen. He was spotted at an erg competition when just sixteen years old by recruiters from Stanford, Dartmouth, Harvard and Brown Universities. As recruiters do, they suggested he apply to their universities with a view to joining 'crew' (American jargon for sweep rowing). He'd won the competition even though it was only his third time on the erg. Having been flown out to these various universities, Jake ultimately settled on Stanford, just under an hour's drive south of San Francisco.

'Rowing at Stanford was far more aggressive than anything I'd done so far. If you didn't win, it was because you hadn't worked hard enough and so the natural solution would be to row harder – the programme there taught me a lot about what it means to train and compete, and the sheer audacity required to strip away the bullshit we use to protect ourselves and be honest about what we really are. In rowing the worst thing you can be is an imposter – if you are, you will be found out ...'

It's an attitude that Jake carries around with him still, and that ultimately might secure him a seat in the Blue Boat. For Duncan promised him a retrial should he make a significant step up rowing-wise. I remember him confronting Jake on the white pontoon in Banyoles immediately after his dismal set of seat-races:

'It's not working for you on bow side, is it?'

'Nope.'

'Want to go back to stroke side and try that instead?'

'Can do—'

'Alright ... let's see how much progress you and Colin can make over the next few weeks. If you can impress us, we might allow you another seat-race in late January.'

Jake, I remember, just stood there like a pillar of salt, eyes glued to his sandals, his mind past reason, past coherence.

The source of all tears had suddenly sprung open within him, black, deep and hot, and they were pouring out and convulsed his body, bending his stubborn head, bowing his shoulders, twisting his face ... His efforts to collect himself were useless. The great knot of ill and grief in his throat swelled upward and he gave in utterly and held his face and wept. He cried with all his heart.[23]

CHAPTER 25

Friday, 12 January

Going is tough this morning. The wind fierce and cold and right to the bone. Given the plentiful rainfall of late, the water is higher than usual, faster-flowing and ferrying all sorts of debris downstream: plastic bags, fags, logs, balloons, newspapers, tampons. Even the van ride to Ely this morning has none of the high-spirited nature of Banyoles. Kip and Dan are the only ones to carry on a conversation at the back of the van. The rest sit wired into their iPods.

Rowing today is a chore too. Gone are the inviting blue-green waters of Banyoles and back is the milky tea of East Anglia's River Great Ouse; 'the colour of rivers that run through cities'.[24] The skies too are sombre and grey. The battle in this nasty, early part of the year is as much psychological as physical, if not more so. Goldie ventures out in two coxed fours. The Blue Boat make do with four pairs, Marco with a single. Bakes makes it clear that he expects a no-nonsense outing. He's in a bad mood, he says, and a good row may help improve his spirits; and off they go.

Once past Adelaide Bridge, the two fours are commandeered into a 5-kilometre side-by-side race, rating 19. In the strong wind, the left side of the river is a more sheltered place to be, and *les misérables* on the right bank are facing a gruesome battle just to keep moving. By the time we reach the midway point, Don has completely lost it. He yanks at his oar in frustration, pulling it straight out of its collar.

'Okay chaps, we'll swap stations here!' Bakes shouts through his megaphone.

The water close to the sheltered riverbank provides a nice boost for Don's crew, allowing them to push ever so slightly ahead. Bakes instructs the other crew to up the rating by two pips. Even with this increased rating, however, they are still barely able to kick a dent in Don's lead. Colin, his lungs now bursting, calls out to Jake (two seats behind him) for what seems to be another strong push. Jake, having already pushed as hard as he can, now loses it.

'Shut the fuck up! Shut the fuck up! *Shut the fuck up!*' he screams, jumping up and off his seat. For a moment I worry that he might actually reach forward and plough his fist into the back of Colin's head. Colin turns eerily silent. He seems confused too. What Jake thought was a criticism of him not working hard enough had been a request from Colin for him to call for another push; for the coxswain, he, Jake and the other two oarsmen had repeatedly called for strong pushes yet none were more effective than Jake's. Yet as far as Jake was concerned, all he could hear was Colin calling out 'Jake' and 'push' in close proximity. It was an innocent misunderstanding that all too easily escalated into an argument, fuelled by a self-conscious insecurity that hangs about perpetually like the scent of sick. By the time we finish the stretch, and Bakes calls for the crews to ease off, it's apologies all round. The guys are clearly still sore after finding themselves at the short end of the stick in selection. In that sense Goldie is united in one respect: every oarsman failed to make the Blue Boat.

Bakes, however, is not unhappy. Being forced to row in the most exposed part of the river and facing a fierce headwind, mental toughness becomes vitally important. To that extent, the outing has been telling. Both crews, when behind, started to row worse rather than better. Instead of cleaning up their act and focusing on tidy, powerful, synchronised and rhythmic rowing, they resorted to doing their own thing: pulling hard in the hope that their unco-ordinated effort might help bridge the distance. And, as Bakes later explains, the more uncoordinated the crew become, the more they start to fight the rhythm and slow the boat down.

Back in Cambridge, Bakes sends round a link to a YouTube clip of Mohammad Ali fighting George Foreman in 1974, with the following attachment:

FIGHTING APPROACH

So this is the kick-off for the Goldie 07, still selection ongoing but this is the group that will make up the final 8+ and I want to start this term with a different approach than some of you may be used to.

I want you to think of yourselves as Fighters. Not just in a general term, I want you to model yourselves on actual fighters, the main example being Muhammad Ali. Before his fights in his body language and his talk you see the confidence he has in what he is about to do. The fear is there but it is masked by his arrogance which is his way of masking it to himself. Personal self talk is a very powerful tool and you must practise it every day you train. Ali actually abuses and taunts his opponents which I certainly won't encourage, but you must Back Yourself and I need to see that in your body language and talk in your own boat before and during every session, but especially when you're about to do something competitive. The World Champion Canadian 8+ used to bang the side of the boat and shout and scream before they raced. I saw this in Duisberg regatta one year and it was an awesome and almost scary sight, they went on to get clear water on the Germans after 400m or so. Very impressive and probably not what I want this crew to do but I want you guys to be different, to take some risks and be the hardest and most ready fighters for the battle on April 7th.

Every fighter takes a good beating at some point and you have the Blue Boat to race so you need to come up fighting every time. I want you to be ready for anything in training and relish the fact that I will be pushing you in every area. When I ask you to jump over a wall I expect the answer in your body language to be 'how high?'

'The fight is won or lost far away from witnesses, behind the lines, in the gym, and out there on the road, long before I dance under those lights.' Muhammad Ali.

RDB

Wednesday, 17 January

From: O.V. De-Groot
To: Russ Glenn
Subject: Training
Date: 17 Jan 2007 22:44
Cc: Tom James, Thorsten Engelmann, Sebastian Schulte, Peter Champion, Kip McDaniel, Kieran West, Dan O'Shaughnessy

Hey guys,

I thought the chat on Sunday was a good first step in figuring out how we want to achieve the most from our training over the next 3 months. Without wanting to make the chat too long, I decided to write down a few points I wanted to make.

In September, Tom remarked that the last two Cambridge Blue Boat crews have been incredibly fast but have failed to perform on the day. *This is crucial*. I'm pretty sure this crew is going to find a lot of speed this year, but again if we fail to perform on the 7th April it's all a waste of time.

I know quite a few of you have read 'Assault on Lake Casitas' by Brad Lewis, and I hope the rest of you will too (Mark has a copy). The thing that stands out is this guy's complete confidence in delivering his best performance on race day. (This doesn't mean he always won, just that when he lost he could not think of anything else that he could have done.) This confidence came from a *lot* of mental preparation off the water, especially shadow rowing with his team-mate. The main goal is to teach yourself total focus and concentration. Nothing could break his focus from rowing his rhythm when distracting things happen on the start line or when his opponent took an unexpected lead.

If there is something that is going to stop us from performing on Boat Race day it is lack of total concentration. I don't think on Boat Race day, our crew concentration and focus towards our goals becomes better just because it's the big day. There is a lot to distract us and I think we need to practise this shadow rowing, going through scenarios and improving our crew focus.

Opinions? I'd really like to incorporate this shadow rowing into our preparation. For me, the mock race calls that Russ calls during the last seventeen minutes of an ergo is not particularly helpful for me.

On a second issue, we discussed the idea of race plans on Sunday and it is clear to me that there are differences of opinion to how useful race plans are and what they should include. Seb, you give me the impression that the race plan is not so important to you, just that we find a rhythm that is unsustainable for the other crews and keep moving. (Tell me if this is not quite what you meant.) Whilst, Tom you seem to be looking for a clearer race plan (although open ended), wanting the crew to have a stronger understanding of different scenarios and a toolkit of calls that Russ has for specific things. I think these two different approaches were also clear in the Trial VIIIs.

My point? Simply that I felt on Sunday you two were kind of saying different things about what you want from a race plan, and I think this should be discussed a bit.

See ya tomorrow

P to M

Oli

CHAPTER 26

Thursday, 18 January

Erging is a bore. Today the guys do 75 minutes on the erg: a 45-minute piece followed by a 30-minute piece, rating precisely twenty strokes per minute. The average splits hover somewhere between 1:48 and 1:52, and there's nothing to do except to repeat that same familiar movement: a push away with the legs, followed by the back, and the arms being pulled towards the chest. On the recovery, this movement reverses, with the arms being stretched out, followed by the body pivoting from the pelvis, the knees being lifted, and the whole body coming forward. Aside from dance music pumped into the gym by Russ and his contraption, there is little to distract the mind. So one copes by allowing oneself to be anaesthetised by the monotony and predictability of the movement, the body fully awake, the mind stupid with narcotic dullness.

Long land-training exercises like this are challenging not just because they are boring. They are physically unpleasant. You sit on a hard plastic seat with your feet jammed in black plastic footholds – causing, particularly with bare feet, no end of discomfort. Then there's the extreme tiredness which sets in pretty rapidly – a tiredness so commanding that all you can think about is the sheer pleasure of giving up. Thus you become your own worst enemy, or at least until the first pain barrier has been mounted and things become a little more tolerable physically.

CHAPTER 27

Thursday, 15 February

I arrive at The Goldie at seven o'clock in the evening, a good 30 minutes early for the crew announcement. By tradition, the line-up for the Goldie and Blue Boat crews is announced internally by the President before being repeated in front of the world's media in a few weeks' time. The ground has been prepared, of course. Those who didn't make either crew have already been told of their fate. Some have taken the news badly. Oli no longer speaks to Duncan. Nor do Don and Colin. Marco is disappointed at not having been given another chance to seat-race for a stab at Goldie, seeing as he wasn't feeling well enough to race in Banyoles. Since then he's worked hard at improving his fitness, and felt he deserved another shot. And so tonight's squad will comprise a cocktail of the good and the bad and the downright bitter.

By 25 past the hour, most are assembled in the Captains' Room. Two rows of chairs are facing Tom and, behind him, the now familiar large oak table. Tom begins his long-awaited crew announcement. The room is quiet enough now to hear a pin drop.

'It's been a long time getting here, or a short time, depending on how you look at it. We've done ergs, lifted weights and God knows how many miles at Ely. We've done the Indoor Champs, the Fours Head, Banyoles, Trial Eights, and for the last four or five weeks selection has been in everyone's heads. And it's just seven weeks now until the Boat Race, until we are going out to face Oxford …

'Before announcing the crews I want to share two ideas that I believe in, that I hold dear and try to adhere to. The first one is this: you've still got to earn your seat. Selection may be over but you've still got to earn your seat among the rest of the guys in the boat. From now until the Boat Race, for seven more weeks. And it's in the small things. It is listening to the coaches and picking up straight away, showing your eagerness, not faffing about, studying the video footage at the end of every training session, small things that show to one another that this actually means something to you.

'My second point is about having an attitude of "no regrets". When it comes to Boat Race day you've got to believe – have no doubt or worry – that you've chosen the right blade, that you've got the right kit on, that you trust one another, that you've done everything you can up to that point to make sure you're not going to have any regrets on the day. If you don't, you're not going to trust those around you. So these are the things I believe in, that I use. I believe you'll be a fucking quick crew if you use them too.

'And so without further ado, here are two crews for the 2007 Boat Race. The Blue Boat: coxswain Russell Glenn, Thorsten Engelmann, Sebastian Schulte, Kieran West, myself, Jake Cornelius,* Pete Champion, Dan O'Shaughnessy and Kip McDaniel. In Goldie: coxswain Rebecca Dowbiggin, David Billings, Don Wyper, Wanne Kromdijk, Oli de Groot, Tobias Garnett, Colin Scott, Doug Perrin and Alistair MacLeod.'

'Oh, and those in the Blue Boat will meet for drinks at The Hawks—'

I steal a glance at Jake in the front row. He seems neither happy nor sad, his eyes locked onto the painted names on the oak panelling – aware no doubt of the deflated looks of Colin and Oli behind him.

---

*Jake's stunning progress since Banyoles had warranted a set of seat-races on the River Great Ouse, which Jake had won, beating Oli and Colin. The hardback edition was justly criticised for leaving out details of these important seat-races. Reality is such that the decisive race itself was very matter-of-fact, and fairly quickly dispensed with. As with most things in life, all the stuff that really mattered happened in the preparation for this event, rather than during the event itself.

CHAPTER 28

Saturday, 3 March

Featuring prominently on the Boat Race calendar are 'fixtures' – mock races against top-flight crews. Of two fixtures, one will typically involve a leading international crew – the German national eight for Cambridge's first fixture and Princeton (the US national crew) for Oxford's first. The second will often be raced against a top-tier national crew – Molesey for Cambridge and Leander in the case of Oxford. This choice of top crews is of course deliberate: fixtures are intended to mimic Boat Race conditions, and the stronger the opposition the better prepared Oxford and Cambridge need to be. They are closely monitored by the media and Old Blues alike, both hoping to put wagers on which of the two crews will prove to be the stronger come 7 April.

Today the Blue Boat will race the reigning World Champions as a prelude to the Boat Race. The big Germans Thorsten and Seb (who would have ordinarily rowed with the Deutschlandachter) have been replaced by two other German World Champions to generate some formidable opposition. Our crew, with Thorsten in stroke seat, get the better start and we're soon half a boat-length ahead of Germany. However, as one reporter later described it, 'their opponents gradually fell into a steady rhythm in breezy but not choppy conditions and on a river whose tidal flow had all but disappeared'. And, sure enough, by the end of the Fulham Wall, Germany had pulled level with Cambridge. Our guys pushed hard to gain another third of a length's advantage, but Germany responded and reversed the situation, putting them a third of a length ahead instead.

And it was all in the rhythm. 'The Germans found a slightly easier rhythm to move on from and we were always chasing it from that point,' Duncan would say afterwards. By the time they reached Hammersmith Bridge, Germany's lead had increased to three-quarters of a length, and they continued to pull away from Cambridge. It wasn't until within view of the finishing line that Russ called for a sprint, helping Cambridge to reduce their margin to within a boat length, or the equivalent of three seconds. An admirable effort but not enough to bring home a victory.

This rhythm, or rather lack of it, was rapidly becoming a symptomatic problem within the crew. Here we knew we had the right combination of individuals – a crew that should sweep Oxford under the carpet – and yet they seemed incapable of finding that Boat Race-winning rhythm. Everything from now on – every coaches' meeting, every training session, every single decision, every bit of controversy – would be driven by one objective alone: to be able to quickly settle into a sustainable rhythm and row not as a loosely-tied unit of eight virtuosos but as a single unit, locked into an indestructible human chain.

CHAPTER 29

Sunday, 4 March

It's gone eleven in the morning and last night's bout of partying hasn't worn off. I feel tipsy, light-headed, nauseous, barely able to get out of bed. My mouth is dry and my bowels bloated. Two Ibuprofen tablets followed by two cups of coffee have done nothing to settle either mind or stomach. I haven't drunk this much for many years – and all in the name of ethnography. Unable to stand still without swaying, I lower my boxers to the floor and sit down to take a pee.

As is traditional, fixtures call for celebrations. Hard work must be rewarded. And so, under the cover of ethnography, I was released for the evening by Roxana and joined the boys for a black-tie dinner at the Hawks Club. Civility forbids me to say more about that night, except that I woke up 'with erectile dong that would scare the Whore of Babylon let alone me'.[25]

The next morning I get a text from Dan: 'How are you feeling? My head is killing me!'

I reply: 'Had a fantastic evening! But still reeling from effect of wine. Could barely see this morning.'

He texts back: 'Same here! I knew it was going to be fun, but that was epic!'

You play as you train.

CHAPTER 30

Monday, 12 March

The internal crew announcement out of the way, it's time for the public to find out who will be racing Oxford on 7 April. This formal announcement, always in full view of the media, ordinarily takes place a few weeks after the President has informed the squad. Later today, at a London venue, Tom will formally challenge Oxford University Boat Club President, Robin Ejsmond-Frey, to a race from Putney to Mortlake. By the time we get to Putney, our corporate sponsor, Xchanging, is ready and waiting with sufficient Boat Race gear to equip a small army.

After the traditional photo-shoot on the banks of the Thames, we walk the 150 or so yards along the Putney embankment to Winchester House, snake through the gate and into the walled garden, through a white marquee and into the grand house itself. Inside, the hallway is oak-panelled, as are many of the rooms, all of it matching the waxed wooden floorboards. We make our way up a flight of stairs to a large reception room, panelled too but this time painted white with stripes in an unmistakeable Cambridge blue.

The room is set up to accommodate the large media presence, with several rows of chairs and the customary aisle separating them. There are large metal contraptions to hold strong lights to aid the camera crews, and in front a makeshift background featuring the sponsor's logo and two oversized television screens. ITV's sports commentator Peter Drury introduces the Challenge to what will be Boat Race number 153, and calls the two Presidents, Tom and Robin, to come forward to introduce their crews.

The formal proceedings over with, but both the Oxford and Cambridge crews still seated in two halves of a semi-circle at the front of the makeshift podium, Oxford oarsman Adam Kosmicki digs into a plastic shopping bag and retrieves a grey-blue toy dolphin. His crew are amused, clearly aware of the exchange that's about to take place. Kosmicki holds the two-foot-long toy by its tail and hands it to fellow Harvard oarsman Kip. The two exchange a few words, inaudible to the rest of us, though I rather suspect this gesture may have something to do with a rare sighting of a dolphin on the Tideway by Duncan last week. While following the crew in his Tin Fish, a dolphin surfaced – and resurfaced – alongside the yellow shell, accompanying it for a good four or five minutes. 'I'm not a local,' Duncan would later tell the press, 'but I imagine that must be pretty rare.' Rare enough anyway for Oxford to present Cambridge with the plastic trophy.

Little did they know then – little did anyone know – that this dolphin sighting was to resurface and play an important role on 7 April.

As for its two-foot inflatable cousin, we duct-taped it to the roof rack of one of our white vans, where it remained until Boat Race day.

As the media descends upon two starry-eyed Boat Race crews, it's interesting to watch seasoned oarsmen like Kip and Kieran being far more comfortable in their skins than relative newcomers like Jake and Pete. From today the media will be following their every movement more carefully than at any time over the past six months. Broadsheets will be eagerly consumed over breakfast, each crew member wondering whether they made today's news. Kip pens his reaction in his online blog:

Sports stars, rowing-style

By: Kip McDaniel

Beginning today and lasting for one month, the rowers of Cambridge and Oxford get to feel like actual sport stars.

It is now officially Boat Race season in England. With this morning's crew announcement, four weeks of media exposure for the 18 young men who will compete on April 7 kicks off. Although the level of attention is still moderate by modern day sporting standards, for us rowers – who toil for decades with an absolutely minimal level of attention focused on us – it is a big deal. It is not too many times in a rowing career that there are five or more video cameras and twice as many photographers snapping at your heels for a few hours.

Going through the media junket this morning that accompanied the announcement of our crews, one thought came to mind: I don't know how professional athletes do it. I'm as vain as the next person, but after three or four interviews, I am thoroughly sick of a) talking about rowing, and b) talking about myself. Yes, I think I can win. No, I am not trying to make up for last year. Yes, Oxford are small and quite ugly. No, I don't think we'll sink. Yes, bow seat is different than stroking. Yes, we'll have pumps this year. After three or four rounds of this, I'm ready for some finger food.

I shouldn't be complaining, of course. Of the thousands of rowers out there, only the smallest of handfuls will have the opportunity to feel like a professional athlete, basking in the moderate glow of media attention for a few weeks. It is just that, as a rower, I have become used to – and, indeed, enjoy – the relative obscurity of our sport.

As rowers, we don't have to put up with post-race press conferences, or read about our team-mates' spats in the newspaper. We don't have to repeat stock answers to boring questions, because 99.9 per cent of the time, no one is asking any. We usually just get to go about our business, training day in and day out and occasionally racing. I do enjoy the interest in the Boat Race, but I have to admit, I would be just as excited to race Oxford on April 7 if no one in the world was watching.

CHAPTER 31

Wednesday, 14 March

Arriving at Goldie at the usual early morning hour, it suddenly dawns on me that the training sessions of late have come to acquire a quite different flavour. No longer is there the usual faffing about, the chit-chat that seasoned the early-morning land training. Instead, the men train in earnest, solemnly focused on a single target approaching them like a freight train, still some distance away but growing larger and more ominous by the minute. The music too is different, barely audible. There's no laughter, no joking, no bantering, just training, and a refreshing gravity and tinge of anticipation. There's something else here now too, something not seen before: a reckless ferocity of purpose.[26]

I finally get a chance to catch up with Dan O'Shaughnessy over coffee at Starbucks. His time with the Club has been somewhat of a rollercoaster ride. Like Jake, he's found it hard to find his bearings – to understand what it was coaches wanted him to do in training. The style of rowing and language used here are very different from those he had grown accustomed to in the US and Canada.

Dan was born in Brockville (Canada) but educated at North-eastern and Syracuse Universities in New York state on rowing scholarships (something which is explicitly forbidden at Oxford and Cambridge, where the Joint Understanding prohibits sporting scholarships for squad members). The sudden loss of his brother to suicide caused him to reflect on the consequences of depression, and probably to overcompensate by adopting a more-positive-than-usual outlook on life. It's one that is greatly appreciated by his fellow oarsmen. Take the Fairbairns Cup race, for example, where Thorsten had relied on Dan to give the normally quiet bow a voice and help the four bow-most oarsmen integrate with the more experienced and far more vocal stern four. They went on to beat their CUBC counterparts by 28 seconds. Dan's vocal efforts were felt to have gone a long way in allowing the crew to settle into a fast and sustainable rhythm. It was here that Dan's contribution first came to the fore in helping move the boat faster, not by means of any individual coup on his part but by drawing a better overall performance out of the rest of them. By helping the crew to lighten up and bond, to be able to find the silver lining around even the gloomiest cloud, Dan seemed uniquely capable of ensuring that the crew would work effectively as a unit. This was something the boys appreciated well before the coaches did – and ultimately would fight them over.

When, during Trial Eights preparation, Dan was swapped from Thorsten's boat into Kieran's, he put his skills to use in what was potentially a problematic crew. Kieran and Seb, as stroke pair, were clearly the most experienced but didn't always see eye to eye. Seb, the younger of the two and a reigning World Champion, had little patience for Kieran's recollections on what worked in the past and why, and why it would be a good idea to try something like it again. Dan's 'I'm too dumb for this – you've got to say this in two sentences or less' seemed effective in reining in Kieran's enthusiasm as well as Seb's aggression. As in Fairbairns, he gave the bow end of the boat a voice, stirring up what had until then been a relatively quiet and inexperienced four oarsmen. And they fared surprisingly well. Even if they still lost, they did so by a mere three seconds over a 4.2-mile course, proving a nice contrast to the Fairbairns difference of 28 seconds over a 2.9-mile course.

What few people had realised until then was the investment Dan made in working his magic to gel the crew socially. As he tells me now, there's many a day when he feels least like being the optimist, the one to fire up the crew and make calls (often told precisely what calls to make by fellow Canadian international Kip McDaniel, seated right behind him). Yet because he knows that it was for principally this reason the returning Blues fought to have him in the boat, he has no option but to force a smile and play the crew comedian.

Before departing for the Christmas holidays, Dan put down a respectable 5,000-metre erg test of 15 minutes 48 seconds, putting him within the six fastest oarsmen and, at least on paper, warranting a shot at the Blue Boat. It's not hard to imagine his disenchantment at being told by Duncan (in Banyoles) that he was still not good enough technically, and wouldn't make the provisional Blue Boat. As soon as Seb got wind of this, he told Tom, who told Thorsten, who told Kip, who told Kieran, until all five returning Blues were fired up and ready to lynch, draw, rack and quarter their coaching team.

Yet the guys knew full well what they were doing. Though Dan was a competent and experienced oarsman, he was technically less adept than Oli or Colin when it came to rowing in that quintessential Cambridge style (sometimes called 'Mahon' style, after the legendary Cambridge finishing coach Harry Mahon). Sometimes it makes sense, even in a context as technically demanding as rowing, to sacrifice some competence to gain likeability; the justification being that of increasing the crew's sociability, not for its own sake but for the crew to achieve that degree of coordination and synchronisation required to achieve maximum boat speed.

There seems to be a rather interesting correlate of this in corporate life. Two American business school academics, Tiziana Casciaro and Miguel Sousa Lobo, in an innovative piece of research, examined trade-off decisions made by managers when given a choice of whom to work with: will they opt for more likeable or more competent individuals, and why? Ask them about this trade-off and they'll tell you that when it comes to getting a job done, technical competence will always trump likeability. After all, it would seem unprofessional not to prefer competence above anything else. Surely this makes sense.

However, their surprise discovery was that, despite what people might say about their preferences, the reverse turned out to be true in practice in the organisations they looked at. Personal feelings played a more important role in forming job-oriented (rather than friendship-oriented) relationships than is commonly acknowledged. If someone is strongly disliked, it's almost irrelevant whether or not they are competent. However, if someone is liked, their colleagues will seek out every little bit of competence they have to offer, a tendency that existed not just in extreme cases but right across the board. As the researchers conclude, a little likeability goes a long way, even in high-performance, technically highly demanding contexts.[27]

CHAPTER 32

Tuesday, 20 March

End of season is beginning to loom larger. Final water session in Ely today. Kip commits the moment to his online blog:

ELY, MAY WE NEVER MEET AGAIN

By: Kip McDaniel

Today was a day of 'lasts'. Tomorrow we leave for London, from where we will go to Chester for a week before returning for the final days before the Boat Race. Today, then, was both the last time I will do a steady state erg and row at our training site in Ely. Ever. Thank God.

This morning was the final erg, seventy minutes of what we call UT2, or, for the layman, of pulling about 1:50 per 500 metres. Over the past two years, I've probably done a hundred of these, if not more. Sitting on the erg, going back and forth, staring out the window at the River Cam or at my monitor. Frankly, I'm glad that my future holds no more of these.

Last steady state erg, you ask? Yes, it's true. Of course, I have hundreds, if not thousands, of kilometres of erging to go until I sleep, as Frost would put it, but no erg workout required of me in the future will be at steady state pace. The reason for this is simple: on the Canadian team, we don't do steady state ergs. We have two relatively simple erg workouts a week, both of which are about 30–40 minutes of full power work at varied ratings. So, for the next year and a half, I am done with steady state erging – unless, of course, I lose my mind and feel like doing one voluntarily.

This afternoon, correspondingly, was my final row on the River Great Ouse, our home training course. To say it is bleak there would be an egregious understatement. Out on the Fens – the vast, flat plains that Cambridge and the surrounding towns sit on – there isn't much to see beyond the occasional church and cow. Few rowing courses can match the monotony of the Ouse.

To send us off, Ely (the name of the town out of which we train) gave us the best it could. As we pushed out, a barrage of hail came down, pelting us hard before we even took a stroke. A heavy wind – by far the stiffest seen all year – drove these clouds away eventually, giving us a brief view of the sun before snow clouds arrived. For the 20 kilometres of rowing done this afternoon (ten into a huge headwind, ten into a correspondingly large tailwind), it snowed for a solid 15. The sun appeared again briefly near the finish before it started to rain. Ely, you will not be missed.

With these two 'lasts' complete, the Boat Race – now less than three weeks away – seems even closer. With a race this weekend versus a top British crew and the Head of the River Thames next weekend, we have clear goals to focus in on. The time, I suspect, will fly by – and I hope it does, because the sooner we can show Oxford how it's done, the better.

Having packed our personal effects in the van and loaded the trailer high with equipment and boats (two eights, two pairs and a single), we lock up one last time and head for the capital. The Blue Boat will row its second and last fixture this weekend on the Tideway. In opposition is Molesey Boat Club, coxed by Oxford coxswain Acer Nethercott and stroked by Andy Hodge, another Oxford Blue and gold medallist in two consecutive World Rowing Championships. Despite formidable opposition, however, it was a race thought to be in Cambridge's favour, with a crew close to peaking and two World Champions of our own and a former Olympic title-holder to boot.

But it was not to be. Cambridge took the lead off the start in a stiff headwind and secured a respectable half-length advantage by the Black Buoy. Rowing past Fulham stadium, however, and with several warnings by the umpire under our belt, Molesey put on the pressure and pulled into a two-thirds lead by the Harrods' Depository. From then on, things went from bad to worse. Even a strong push around the Surrey bend proved futile as Molesey counterattacked and opened up a three-quarter-length overall lead, which they maintained until the finish. The underdogs had got the better of Cambridge in a race which was to have calamitous consequences for one of us.

From: Duncan Holland
To: Donald Legget, Dan O'Shaughnessy, Jake Cornelius, Kieran West, Kip McDaniel, Mark de Rond, Peter Champion, Russ Glenn, Sebastian Schulte, Thorsten Engelmann, Tom James
Subject: P to M
Date: Sat, 24 Mar 2007 09:55:20 -0000

Team,

We have a very clear task ahead of us.

You are an extremely fast crew, the challenge is to express that speed in a tight situation. We know how to go fast, what we are not good enough at is racing. All of you have been fast before and I am absolutely confident this crew can go fast on April 7 and beat OUBC.

What we must do is work together to build a focus and confidence that we can do it when it counts. We don't need to reinvent how to row, we need to trust ourselves, trust one another and build confidence and momentum so you go out on race day knowing how you will row and knowing you can do it.

Let's embrace the task!

Duncan

From: Sebastian Schulte
To: Duncan Holland, Donald Legget, Dan O'Shaughnessy, Jake Cornelius, Kieran West, Kip McDaniel, Mark de Rond, Peter Champion, Russ Glenn, Thorsten Engelmann, Tom James
Subject: Re: P to M
Date: Sat, 24 Mar 2007 10:07:27 +0000

Good calls from Duncan. Couldn't agree more.

We have two weeks to go from today. Two weeks is a lot of time to implement our decent pattern into racing situations.

As Duncan says, there is no need to reinvent the wheel, we just need to recall what we're good in:

1. Strong drive, body swing, leg press and hold the finish
2. Loose catches which allow us always to apply (1)
3. (1) and (2) allows us to accelerate every stroke, and that's all we need
3. Calmness in the race because we know we're good

That's it.

Yesterday, we started aggressively, but after 500m we still hit the catches as we did in the sprint, so we were not able to accelerate. The power goes off, which is natural. Hence, we weren't capable of accelerating anymore.

One of my 'old stories':

2006, Henley. Our crew developed a great pattern, in low and medium rates. However, we didn't implement that pattern against the Dutch and lost. Afterwards, we sat together, drew the conclusions as above, gained confidence and tried it again just a week afterwards in Lucerne, winning the final and beating the fucking Dutch by 10 seconds. Same crew, same pattern, but with a much more clinical approach.

Easy to change, so let's do it. We're still awesome.

Seb

CHAPTER 33

Wednesday, 28 March

Sitting high up on a mountain in Missoula, Montana, I receive a short text from Sebastian, like a bolt out of the blue: 'Rebecca is now in charge of the Blue Boat!'

As I look down on the University of Montana campus below me – its buildings like coloured bits of Lego – I feel a million miles away. My first thoughts are, rather selfishly, with my research. Here we have one of the most significant developments of the year, one that merits documenting in detail, and yet I'm nowhere close to the action. Academic conferences in such placid hideouts as Missoula are invariably popular with scholars, but the timing of this one couldn't have been worse.

My second concern is with Russ. Having felt more or less certain of a place in the Blue Boat this year – after all, he was only recently introduced to the world's media as the 2007 coxswain – he now finds himself bartered for a relative novice to the CUBC. This will have hit Russ like a brick in the face. Try as I might, I cannot imagine the impact of this decision on his spirits. How did he find out, I wonder? And how will Rebecca have reacted? The broadsheets will no doubt be having a field day championing the comparatively inexperienced ginger-haired British female as having staged a coup d'etat by unseating the experienced American at the last possible opportunity, with less than two weeks to go, even as he's told all his friends, his parents and siblings, the Master of his College. Has the CUBC lost its marbles? Is Duncan getting cold feet? Or could this be a tactical move?

As expected, the media are quick to the bat and merciless. As *The Guardian* put it: 'Last-minute changes are not unknown ... in 1993 Oxford switched coxes 10 days before losing. Last year Oxford's Nick Brodie was announced as the Dark Blue cox at the Challenge but demoted a day later ... The decision of the Cambridge coach, Duncan Holland, to change coxes this close to the race has a smack of desperation about it ...'

❖

Arriving by train in Chester two days later, Duncan is waiting for me on the platform. The squad decided to spend their penultimate week at a military base near the Welsh border, some 200 miles away from the Tideway, hoping to train and prepare for the Boat Race without distraction by the media. He invites me to sit down for a coffee at a platform cafe and, as if able to read my mind, comes to the point pretty quickly. Russ, he says, steered badly in the Molesey fixture. In fact, he hasn't been steering all that well since Banyoles and his aggression isn't particularly helpful with a crew as experienced as the Blue Boat. 'He's been trying to race the boat rather than having the crew row the boat,' Duncan volunteers as he takes receipt of two lattes, handing me one.

'Sugar?'

'No thanks.'

'Rebecca's come on nicely despite her lack of experience.'

(Sound of teaspoons twirling.)

As one of identical twins, Rebecca grew up in Cambridge and opted for an International Baccalaureate (rather than A levels) before going up to Emmanuel College to study Anglo-Saxon, Norse and Celtic history. It's here that she acquired a taste for coxing, starting in Emmanuel's novice women's crew and moving on from there to coxing their second women's boat in the Mays of her first year as an undergraduate. Substituting college for university rowing, she trialled successfully with the Cambridge Lightweight rowing team – so called because no oarsman may weigh more than 72.5kg (11st 6lb), and the average weight of the crew (not including the coxswain) must not be greater than 70.0kg (11st) – followed by a season with the university's women's rowing squad. Both the Cambridge University Women's Boat Club (CUWBC) and the Lightweights race not on the Tideway but on a 2,000-metre stretch in Henley-on-Thames in late March or early April, usually a week or so before the Boat Race.

Rebecca had wanted to cox for CUBC and had tried twice, but failed each time to make the cut. It wasn't until her third attempt that she secured herself a place. With hindsight, she herself admits to not having anything near the self-confidence she would have needed to manage a crew of internationals. She was quiet, withdrawn, and seemed afraid of the guys, never quite distinguishing herself as a true contender to cox the Boat Race. Had she, upon returning to CUBC for the third time (now as a PhD student), been offered the chance to cox Goldie, she would have grasped it with both hands. After all, with seven hopefuls trialling for two coxswain positions, the reserve boat would have proved quite a coup. And yet when told in Banyoles that she'd be coxing the provisional Goldie crew, she was enormously disappointed. She had made such progress, or so she thought, and being tied to Goldie would give her no chance to challenge Russ over the Blue Boat. From that moment on, things continued to go downhill as far as she was concerned. It wasn't that she didn't try, or so she tells me later, but because she felt stuck in a vicious cycle of under-performance. The worst bit of it was that her doing so badly would only reinforce Duncan's opinion that he'd been right all along to pick Russ for the Blue Boat. It wasn't until she finally scrambled together the courage to ask Bakes for help that she began to improve and grow in confidence.

The Boat Race requires a near-perfect ability of coxswains to keep a mental note on everything happening in and around the boat. It's about far more than control of a rudder (the size of a credit card), but rather involves an ongoing negotiation between empathy and assertiveness – having to understand what the crew are still capable of doing in a race and daring to make bold decisions and to take responsibility for them. It means communicating with stroke, who has a good visual of the umpire driving some yards behind. Coxing means making calls that actually improve boat speed. It's diplomacy and advocacy and prejudgement and goading, collapsed in a mere 55 kilograms. In the Boat Race there's no room for error: things have got to be perfect, as they very nearly were with Rebecca as cox in Goldie's fixture against London Rowing Club this past weekend – something the race umpire (none other than our Macedonian spear expert and six-time Oxford Blue, Boris Rankov) was sure to point out.

Having arrived in Chester after Goldie's second fixture, she sensed something might be in the air. Duncan, Donald, Grant, Bakes and Tom had isolated themselves for a longer-than-usual summit. She was pretty pleased with her fixture and was aware of criticisms levelled against Russ's recent coxing, but thought no more of it. That is, until half past ten that evening when Tom and Duncan entered her digs.

'We decided to switch coxswains ...'

And there it was. As simple as that. These were the precise words she had imagined herself hearing on many a van ride over the past twelve weeks. And here they were. So this is what it felt like, she thought, the first symptoms of excitement stirring inside her.

Tom, however, looked anything but thrilled. For where there's a winner ... 'I talked to Russ ... He feels pretty sick about it all. But I talked to the guys too and it's what we think is best for the Blue Boat right now. Anyway, that's what we'd come to tell you.'

Duncan added that this decision had not been made lightly, but that the consensus was that she had continued to improve and eventually surpassed Russ, and that these things are never pretty, nor easy, but that it's ultimately their job to do what they think is best for the crew.

'Actually, there's a bit more to it,' Kieran will tell me later. 'Russ coxed poorly in the Molesey fixture and everyone was worried that if he repeated his erratic steering under pressure he could actually lose us the race. On the way to Chester, Seb and I discussed it. Seb asked me whether I thought we should change coxes. I said I thought it was a huge decision to take but that I really did have issues with Russ's inappropriate and unnecessarily aggressive calls, and that we had tried to tell him this. And so that evening in Chester when Duncan broached the subject I said I'd accept changing coxes but only if I knew absolutely for certain that this is what every member of the crew wanted, and that we should all put our honest opinions forward there and then. And so we did. One by one we all spoke up – Kip, Dan, Seb, Thorsten, Jake, Pete – and all pretty much decided that we didn't think his calls were helpful, but that we hadn't said anything because we each thought everybody else liked Russ and so didn't want to cause dissent in the crew. That's pretty much it. That's what happened that evening …'

What neither Kieran nor the crew seem to have realised at the time was that a parallel conversation had been taking place within the coaching team ever since Trial Eights. Martin Haycock, coxswain of the legendary 1993 Cambridge crew and now on the coaching team, had been impressed with Rebecca's rapid improvements. Even when put under significant pressure by Russ in coxing one of the Trial Eight crews, she never gave in nor lost composure – reflecting a quiet inner confidence gradually coming to the fore. But was she improving at a rapid enough pace to outdo the much more experienced American?

Having coxed for Cambridge, Nottinghamshire County, and London Rowing Club, Martin had been invited back to CUBC in 2006 as a coxswain advisor. It's a role he shares with Chris Drury, guru of Tideway tactics, who was to play a vital role in formulating Cambridge's race plan. Seeing Russ fare poorly in both of his fixtures, yet Rebecca steering a near-perfect line in her second mock race, an idea that seemed crazy just three months ago suddenly struck a chord. What if she were handed the reins of the Blue Boat? Would she be able to manage the likes of Kieran, Seb and Kip? Technique aside, is she sufficiently strong-spirited?

Martin, over the last twelve weeks in particular, had reassured

Rebecca repeatedly that she ought never to give up hope of making the Blue Boat, no matter how far into the season. After all, he was a late recruit himself. After turning the tide on Oxford in 1993, he had failed to make the cut for the 1994 crew and, had it not been for a terrible first fixture by his chief rival for the coxswain seat, he may not have made the 1994 Blue Boat at all. So Martin knew full well what it felt like to be battling against the odds, but also how fickle and unpredictable the road towards Boat Race history can be.

From: Martin Haycock
To: R.M. Dowbiggin
Subject:
Date: 21 December 2006 18:57

The pressure of the BR is of a different magnitude from any race you will ever do. From what I gather an Olympic final is a close match! Prove you're made of the sort of stuff that marks you out as one of life's winners.

Think of it in two ways a) protecting your downside b) proving your flair. Key to (a) is not to make any mistakes or do anything stupid. Examples are hitting buoys, crashing into landing stages, calling wrong times or not doing the exercise you've been asked to do. You should aim to be building a picture of yourself as utterly reliable and unflappable.

The key to (b) is identifying those critical outings and moments, and making smart decisions at the right time, just like that key call you made around Chiswick Steps in Trial VIIIs. If seat-racing, realise who is being tested and how it might be affecting them. Put yourself in the shoes and minds of the athletes and think where you can add value.

One of the keys I think to handling the pressure is to be loving every minute of it. If you are visibly enjoying yourself and the boat's going well it will rub off. It's a bit like the idea that people can tell if you're smiling down the phone. To be over-serious and insular and stressed won't help (even if that's what's happening inside!). You've done the hard bit and earned respect from some world class athletes. You are not the sort of person to fall into complacency, so afford yourself some pats on the back, stand proud without being cocky and approach outings as an equal to all the others out there.

Put it this way: TJ, Thorsten, Seb, Kip. None of those guys have ever won the BR before. Neither have you. So you're equal in my (Boat Race) eyes!

Seems to me you're on top of the issues. My main advice is just to be yourself, enjoy yourself in this amazing club of ours and let the talent you know you have become increasingly evident to the group.

Martin

Martin's brief to Rebecca serves as a small but important window into a parallel universe where Old Blues and coaches gather to think and argue and plan. It's a macrocosm more obscure and inaccessible even than the everyday microcosm of the squad – one that, despite its obscurity, protects and forever safeguards that sacred tradition of Varsity rowing. It's the mother cradling the child.

The first outing as a reconfigured Blue Boat passes remarkably smoothly. So, incidentally, does Goldie's. The upshot of this affair, however agonising and painful for Russ, is that both crews seem to feel they have the better coxswain. Russ's assertiveness is ideal for Goldie's less experienced oarsmen. Rebecca's serenity, by contrast, works wonders for the internationals.

Later that week, Russ drops by her room too, with 'Congratulations ... I'm sure you'll do a great job,' before retiring into relative obscurity.

The decision to swap coxswains this late in the season was but one of two issues hovering like rain clouds over the squad. Duncan decided to temporarily swap Kieran into stroke position and move Thorsten to 6 seat ('to try out a new configuration, that's all,' Duncan had said). It's all part of the rhythm puzzle – of locating that missing element to help the crew settle into a fast and sustainable rhythm early on in the race. So far that rhythm has proved, well, elusive. Seb, however, is having none of it.

'Kieran's fine and makes a great stroke at lower ratings, and he may be the best pairs partner one could wish for, but Thorsten's a better racing stroke and all Duncan's doing is messing with the crew order and unsettling them and causing them to row badly and just making a big mess of things ... I'll have a word with Tom about it. You don't swap a new guy into stroke this late in the game ... What the bloody hell does Duncan think he's doing?'

Listening to Seb rant, I'm reminded of how fragile relationships are, of how even after six long months the crew are still swayed by suspicions of hidden agendas and ulterior motives, seeing the worst in everyone and everything. So why is the default position when things fall to bits invariably that of second-guessing some-one else's intentions? Is there anything more alienating or offen-sive? What would happen if we were to accept that reality is often far more benign, more innocent than the paranoid worlds we tend to construct for ourselves?

❖

Our barracks in the Welsh borders provide only the basics of com-fort. The beds have iron frames and fishnet springs to support a three-inch foam mattress. On top lies a scratchy horsehair blanket, rough to the touch and, it seems, cut from the same cloth as the carpet under my feet. (It even has the same colour.) Opposite me, as I sit on the bed writing, are two wardrobes but no hangers. Above the bed and on the wall hangs a small fluorescent tube, punching well above its weight. The curtains, cobalt blue with delicate decorations in gold trim, look oddly out of place. Staring about the room, I realise as never before that I am alone. Having spent every waking hour of every day over the past six months with the squad, I feel lonely and isolated here in this small empty room at the end of the corridor. I grab my stuff and move in with Jake and Thorsten, sleeping, as they do, on mattresses on the floor.

'So where were you when the shit hit the fan?' Jake asks.

'Yeah, you leave and everything falls to pieces,' adds Thorsten.

After a half-dozen games of Asshole (a card game popular with the boys, courtesy of Jake), we make our beds, kill the big fluorescent ceiling lights and turn on the smaller but no less bright reading lights, grab a book each, and stretch out across our foam mattresses. Thorsten and Jake are deeply absorbed in *The Game* – a controversial book based on the premise that women can be manipulated like Play-Doh from the bar into the sack. Courtesy of Neil Strauss, the method is now available from any decent bookstore for just short of nine quid.

> One of the world's greatest mysteries is the mind of a woman … So I set out to solve it. … [T]he key is to ignore the woman you desire while winning over her friends – especially the men and anyone else likely to cockblock. If the target is attractive and used to men fawning all over her, the pickup artist must intrigue her by pretending to be unaffected by her charm. This is accomplished through the use of what he called a neg. Neither compliment nor insult, a neg is something in between – an accidental insult or backhanded compliment. The purpose of a neg is to lower a woman's self esteem while actively displaying a lack of interest in her – by telling her she has lipstick on her teeth, for example, or offering her a piece of gum after she speaks. 'I don't alienate ugly girls; I don't alienate guys. I only alienate the girls I want to fuck.'[28]

Jake (to Thorsten): 'Bro, what page you on in the bang book?'
Thorsten: 'One-thirty-two – you?'
Jake: 'Four-seven-oh – damn interesting, ain't it?'
Thorsten sniggers.
It's nice to be back.

CHAPTER 34

Thursday, 29 March

After a restless night I wake up famished. Breakfast consists of a choice between a traditional fry-up, cereal, or toast and jam. The fry-up looks unappetising: slices of fried white bread, greasy sausages, black pudding, fried slices of bacon, fried tomatoes and baked beans, the tin tray of scrambled egg already empty. Everything feels a little cheap: the orange juice is orange drink, the strawberry jam is strawberry jelly, the yoghurt watery. So this is what a soldier's fare is like, I think, increasing my esteem for the poor bastards being paid next to nothing for risking everything in some forlorn fuckhole in Iraq or Afghanistan.

I grab a seat opposite Jake at the breakfast table. He looks more pensive than usual.

'Read that book?' He points at his thumbed copy of *The Game*.

'Nope. Well, actually, about a third of it. Found it, I don't know, uncomfortable—'

'Too bad you didn't finish it,' Jake mumbles between toast, 'because at the end of it things start to get all fucked up and I think it really does come down on the side of "Okay, you can't treat people like that or you'll be miserable."'

(Buttering his next piece ...)

'They all start playing these fucking mind games with each other and all the experienced pick-up artists are forced to face up to the fact that they can't form relationships with anybody. So it's not really all that disturbing. It's actually quite self-conscious about what it wants to do. It reinforces the idea that people are

183

means not ends, stuff to be bought and sold and used and chucked out – life at its most hollow.'

I look up at Jake in surprise.

'In some way it also shows how the things we think we want won't make us happy. I mean every guy who reads that book does so because he wants to learn how to get girls in the sack easier. But by the end of the book it's obvious that doing so has a real cost too, and until we learn that what we want right now isn't what we want in the long term we keep making mistakes that make us depressed.

'I mean, look at rowing. There are extremely compelling reasons to stop during a race, and in almost every race I can remember I've thought to myself "If only I could stop rowing I would never want anything again. I would rest forever. I don't care what the consequences are of my stopping. Nothing can be as bad as this." But the reasonable part of your brain says "Don't stop. It won't make you happy. If you stop you will never forgive yourself." In rowing you need to cultivate that instinct, you need to practise to make the second voice louder than the first, and it's the same in the rest of life. And in that sense, inasmuch as the book is a cautionary tale about what happens if we pursue what we think we want, I think it's a really good book actually—'

(I'm lost for words.)

Later that morning I watch from the boathouse as the crew pull in, undo their rowing shoes, get out and put the oars and boat away. The mood is glum and hangs about like a thick fog. My suspicions that this may have something to do with the crew line-up are reinforced on our return journey to the barracks. As we walk from the car park, Seb turns around to face us. He wants a meeting, he says, to discuss what he thinks is an ill-fated attempt to sneak Kieran into stroke seat. Making changes this close to the race is plain stupid, and do Duncan and Donald not realise that everyone knows what tricks they're up to? As far as he can see, it's a bloody conspiracy.

I try telling him that, having sat in on nearly every coaching meeting, I haven't seen any evidence of hidden agendas, that everyone genuinely seems to be doing their best, that the optimal configuration of the boat is still far from obvious. The fastest combination is just not easy to find, even if obvious to him. Seb, however, remains unconvinced.

The conversation continues in our room. Thorsten, sitting on his mattress with his knees pulled up, gets emotional when talking about his role in the boat. He feels badly about having lost their two fixtures as stroke man – which is why he thinks Duncan is swapping Kieran in and him out – and feels paralysed, unable to complain or criticise Kieran's rowing. It would inevitably be seen as 'sour grapes' on his part, wouldn't it? – as him furthering his own interests and making the rowing worse for everyone deliberately by rowing sub-optimally, and so setting Kieran and the crew up for failure. He feels confused. After all, why did Duncan tell him that he would be returned to stroke seat after two outings, and yet tell him this morning that Kieran will remain in stroke seat for the time being? What is he supposed to think?

'It's all so damn confusing—'

Tom decides to raise the issue that afternoon in the boathouse gym. Everyone's on edge, knowing this issue could as easily destroy as bring the crew together. On his prompt, we sit ourselves down on various pieces of equipment. I park myself on one of the ergs. So does Kip. Kieran and Tom share one of two wooden benches. Donald and Duncan share the other and, having placed theirs at a 90-degree angle from Tom and Kieran's, complete the circle.

'I want each of you to tell me how you think the outing felt this morning, and not worry about what it might mean for either Thorsten or Kieran,' Tom begins. 'I simply want everyone to be completely honest so we can settle this thing and move on ...'

'Thorsten's rhythm feels more sustainable than Kieran's. Sorry Kieran.' Seb has taken the bite. Kip agrees. Donald does not.

'As far as I can see, Kieran looks better at stroke.'

'What do you mean?' Thorsten mumbles unhappily.

'Just like I said, I think Kieran looks better at stroke.' Duncan nods in agreement. Thorsten looks downcast. Little did I realise at the time – little did anyone know – how close he was then to walking out of the gym and out of the squad. 'I desperately wanted to walk out right there and then and leave them to it to row the race by themselves,' he would say in our room afterwards, still angry and annoyed. The atmosphere remains tense as we sit around quietly, uncomfortably.

'Okay, here's a way forward—' Kieran looks agitated. 'To be honest I don't know why we're having this conversation now. So far as I know, the reason I've been in the stroke seat for the last two days is to give Thorsten a bit of a break and a chance to feel the rhythm further down the crew. I never asked to stroke this crew and this close to the Race I don't want the stroke seat. Maybe back in January but not today … Actually I'm pretty pissed off we're having this meeting at all. The only thing that should matter at this point is how we can make this boat go as fast as possible, not who sits where. It's not about some glory seat or any of that crap, but whether or not we win next week – and if we do, nobody will give a shit who sat where; and if we lose, no one will give a shit either who was at stroke – and so long as we win, I don't care who sits where. If I'm told that sitting in the bow seat will make the boat go faster, I'll go there; I'll even cox the bloody thing if that's what it needs …'

Kieran's outburst is hitting its intended target. He's got our attention.

'For goodness' sake, it really isn't just up to stroke to set the boat rhythm; it's up to each and every one of us, so at the end of the day it makes fuck all difference whether Thorsten or I sit at the front; we have all got to take collective responsibility for the boat moving together so please let's stop fucking around and wasting time worrying about who sits where and concentrate on what we can each do to influence the boat speed. That applies to everyone equally: me, Thorsten, Pete, Tom, whoever … So Thorsten sits at stroke, I'm at six, we all stop worrying about what everyone else is doing and fucking well concentrate on our individual jobs! That way we'll win this bloody race and none of this will matter. Problem solved!'

Tom gets up, grabs his drink bottle and turns towards the door.

'Good call, Kieran. Let's get on the water and do this. Let's go and win this fucking race!' He is followed hard on his heels by Thorsten, Seb, Kip, Kieran, Dan, Jake, Pete and Rebecca. Duncan and Donald never do get a chance to contribute any closing statements. Nor are they any longer expected to make any decisions. The crew have effectively taken things into their own hands.

The boat belongs to them now.

CHAPTER 35

'Want to have a chat?' Kip saunters into our bedroom, his dark curly hair matted from a recent nap. The boys often catch up on sleep between outings.

'Sure.'

'Want one of these too?' He raises the bottle in his hand.

Armed with a Stella each, we walk and we talk. The breeze outside is refreshing. The scent of recently cut grass suits the view of sheep and rolling hills in front of us. Like a picture postcard, the countryside is all calm and serenity. For me at least. The handsome, curly-haired Canadian is feeling rather less peaceful.

'I can't fucking believe it ... We had the best-ever row on Tuesday and then Duncan decides to swap Thorsten and Kieran, which upset everything. Even assuming it makes sense from a technical perspective to swap the two, it makes no sense from a psychological perspective. None whatsoever. It's just plain stupid. The last thing you want to do in approaching a race is to upset the boat. We've already had a last-minute change of coxswain – and now there's this ...!'

A prodigy of Harvard coach Harry Parker, one of the most successful coaches in US collegiate history, Kip was raised in Cobble Hill, British Columbia, in privileged surroundings. Aged twelve, his parents sent him to Shawnigan Lake School, a private boarding school 45 minutes north of Victoria on the idyllic Vancouver Island, where he first took up rowing. His brother had taken to the water a few years earlier, and before that his father had rowed for Canada. The choice of rowing, in other words, was straightforward. At

Harvard, Parker suggested that Kip try his hand at stroking the boat – a place which he occupied throughout his four-year rowing career there, during which he saw off several strong university crews, including Yale in the American equivalent of the Boat Race.

After graduating with a Bachelor's degree in Government, Kip took a year out to pursue a career as a financial journalist on Wall Street, gaining a considerable amount of weight in the process. Dissatisfied both with his choice of career and rapid weight gain, he decided to resume rowing full-time, gave his employer the required two weeks' notice, and left New York City for Boston. Within six weeks, Kip had dispatched 45 pounds of bodyweight (by making sure he consumed fewer calories than he burned on the erg). In fact, having committed himself to a strenuous two one-hour erg sessions per day plus weights, plus water training, he was barely able to catch a proper night's sleep during his first week of training. Despite the physical discomfort, however, Kip fondly remembers this as an exciting time, one focused on a singular objective – to try to make the Canadian national squad.

Where there's a will there's a way, or there was in his case any-way. He made it into the national squad and went on to win a World Championships bronze medal in 2005. Having stroked some very successful crews, Kip would have seemed an obvious candidate to stroke the Blue Boat again this season. He has the aggression expected of a stroke, and the experience to go along with it. However, the Boat Race result of last year, which saw Cambridge fall five lengths behind, will almost inevitably rule this out. Partly due to this experience, partly because his lower back problems had worsened, and partly because he figured he'd stand a better chance of being selected as a bow-sider, Kip asked to change from rowing at the stern to rowing on bow side. This effec-tively meant that he spent the best part of two weeks getting used to rowing with the oar to his left rather than his right. The Fours Head was to be his baptism of fire as bow-man.

The run-up to this race proved a low point in Kip's Cambridge career. He was passed over for the first, and even the second-best crew, despite being one of the five most experienced racers. Thorsten, Kieran, Tom and Seb had been put together in what Duncan liked to call the 'big four'.

'I wasn't even thought good enough for the second four. That really pissed me off. I felt I was being lied to by the coaches because they kept telling me that it really was the second-best boat, whereas it was obvious that it wasn't. I mean, don't bullshit me by trying to make me feel good about being in a crew when I jolly well know, as does everyone else, that it's not one of the better boats. I'm one of five international oarsmen and yet was made to feel like I was somehow inferior to the rest.

'And this carried on into the Banyoles training camp. I was being seat-raced with everyone else except the "big four". They were doing steady-state rowing while I was being seat-raced fourteen times a day ... I mean, even if those four would have easily won every seat-race, they should be raced at least once just to show the rest of the guys that they've actually earned their place in the squad – to show everyone that they're good enough to be here.

'And then there's the way the boat was being coached, with everything focused on the bow four, making sure that we wouldn't do anything to disrupt the "perfect" rowing of the stern four; that we were somehow the runt of the crew that needed help – that just felt bloody awful.'

So Kip fought back. His Fours Head crew, though unpromising on paper, beat what was effectively the second-best boat. And on the 5,000-metre erg test, he easily put himself within the top four bow-siders and beat the next best oarsman in seat-racing to leave sufficient space between him and other hopefuls.

The current Blue Boat, he thinks, is approaching an ideal eight in psychological terms. The guys are serious about racing and yet the mood retains a light touch. This is partly the result of Dan and him pulling out all the stops to make sure the stern four remain happy, 'because when they're happy they're some of the best bloody rowers in the world. You've got to be quietly confident and relaxed about the race when going into it. There's absolutely no need for an overly serious attitude, and so Dan and I tell jokes to try and keep the mood light. On race day we should be nervous as hell but also have that all-important sense of relaxation, being able to joke a little while taking the boat out. Now that would be ideal ... Oh, and of course for the coaches to tell us on the eve of the Boat Race that there's nothing more they can tell us, that we've done all the work and that if only we row as we've trained to row, we will do very well.

'The guys in the boat this year are happier than last year, or seem to be in any case. Last year Seb was desperate to sit where Tom was sitting. Kieran, I suspect, is happier with Thorsten than me at stroke. And, hey, if he's a happier oarsman, he'll row better. Pete and Jake enjoy being in 3 and 4. I like being behind Dan and sharing responsibility for keeping the rest of the crew happy. Things just feel right this time somehow.'

Whether that's enough remains, of course, to be seen.

CHAPTER 36

Friday, 30 March

We hurtle down the black asphalt en route to the metropolis and its river for the final few days of Boat Race preparation. For the next eight nights we will be staying in comfortable surroundings in Victorian Putney, with dedicated cooks, wireless internet, a TV and DVD player, fussball, table tennis, and a selection of broadsheets every morning, the point being to supply the crews with an environment that is wholesome, relaxing, and remarkably free of worry.

Duncan, Donald and Grant will eat with the crew once daily but otherwise stay put in a house nearby, allowing Rebecca and the guys to bond as a crew. Goldie has its own place, just as luxurious and comfortable. The crew are assigned upstairs rooms; two to a room except for Rebecca, who gets her own digs. For lack of space I'm relegated to a saggy, moth-holed sofa which stands like a sack of potatoes in the downstairs living room. It should turn into a double bed with a few practised moves. The room smells of beeswax and furniture, and showcases an assortment of prints and family portraits, a large desk facing sash windows, two small but well-stocked wooden bookcases, a large gold-framed mirror above a small writing desk, and, beneath it all, a soft green carpet, nice to the touch. A larger room next door accommodates two flowery sofas facing each other, a coffee table with the fussball game on top, various antiques, potted plants here and there, and large windows facing the back garden. As I unpack my bags for the second

192

time in four days, it finally dawns on me – today is the beginning of the last week before the Boat Race.

We sit down to a home-cooked dinner of shepherd's pie, broccoli and string beans, topped off with apple crumble and ice cream. There is a strict embargo on fizzy drinks and alcohol. Food-wise we can request whatever we like, the only proviso being that it must be wholesome and prepared by our cooks (who truly are first-class, and charming besides). The dinner table conversation is dominated by tomorrow's Head of the River Race which, like the Fours Head, will be rowed with the outgoing tide on the Championship course. To have decided to participate in this race just a week before the Boat Race is to take a very serious risk. It could prove detrimental to the crew's physiology, not just because the race is physically demanding, but because it could cause the crew to peak too early. On the upside, if they do well, it will be a tremendous boost to their confidence. And a terrible blow to Oxford's.

Saturday, 31 March

Despite comfortable surroundings, I sleep badly. The sofa bed proved too short and left my feet and ankles dangling out of reach of the duvet. Even now they feel cold and numb. When, after 22 pages of *The Game*, I finally did fall asleep, I was tormented by dreams, each more alarming than the one before.

I'm the last to wake up, and might not have woken at all had it not been for Pete's 'Morning Mark. Ten minutes till Duncan comes to pick us up. Thought you'd like to know.'

(Fuck.)

With the Head Race to prepare for, the crew are unusually focused. Even Donald is pleased at the morning's outing on the Tideway. It's the best rowing he's seen so far, he says. All should bode well for the afternoon race except that the weather seems to be taking a turn for the worse. The wind has picked up, as have the waves, and the water beyond Hammersmith Bridge looks frighteningly similar to that of the 2006 Boat Race, when Cambridge took on so much water that it made racing virtually impossible.

'We'll put in the pumps this time,' Duncan decides. Grant and he will stay behind to make sure the battery-operated pumps are bolted in, charged, and working. Whatever happens, there will not be a repeat of last year, when Oxford's pumps prevailed over Cambridge's want of them. And so we take off without Duncan and Grant on our short drive back to the house for a wholesome pasta lunch, a shower, a 'nap and a crap'.

Walking back from the upstairs bathroom, I catch a glimpse of Jake through a crack in his bedroom door. He rests on the edge of his bed stark naked, elbows resting on his knees, hands folded in his lap. It's a telling image. Even if today's race is a minor event compared to next weekend's, it's likely to have a big impact on the crew. Should things go well, it will allow them to finally set aside the memories of last year's anguish. If not, it will invariably destroy whatever is left of their already fragile confidence, leaving them worse off than had they not raced. It's a massive risk physiologically as well as psychologically.

We arrive at the KCS boathouse 30 minutes before pushing off. The boat has been polished, the sun is out, but the wind has picked up speed. Already there's talk of the race being cancelled. I wander about with nothing much to do while the guys get changed and stretch. Kip, as usual, stands isolated from the rest of the crew and listens to his iPod, hands cupped over his earphones. Tom paces the boathouse nervously. Jake is lying face-down on the massage table while Linda is busily kneading his hamstrings. Dan and Pete sit on the floor stretching, each sharing one half of a single set of headphones plugged into Pete's MP3 player. Rebecca has parked herself on one of the metal chairs facing the boys, her back against the window. She looks nervous too. And who wouldn't? After all, this will be her litmus test.

'Cox-box charged?'

'Yes.'

'Headset?'

'Check.'

'Tools?'

'Yup.'

'Okay boys, the plan is simple,' Duncan continues. 'Race as you want to race next weekend. Find your rhythm and stay in it no matter what else is happening around you. Keep your eyes in your own boat, and row your own race.'

'Duncan's right,' Tom says. 'The conditions out on the water are rough, much like they were last year actually. But it's good practice. No one knows what the river will look like seven days from now anyway. And remember that Molesey is racing ahead of us, so it's our chance to redeem ourselves from last week's fixture. So let's go for them big time.'

Donald coughs before speaking up. He stands behind the boys, hands in his pockets. 'Frankly, I must admit that I didn't think entering the Head was a good idea. I was against it and I told Tom so. However, seeing the progress you've made in just two weeks, and seeing how well you rowed this morning, I now think it a jolly good idea. You're rowing the best you have so far. And this time last year you were going backwards rather than forwards. So,' he wheezes, 'good luck.'

Spurred on, the crew commit their boat to the water and push off.

Having seen them off, I walk the mile and a half or so to Hammersmith Bridge and find myself a spot among the crowds gathered there. Walking past Harrods' Depository I can already see the bridge packed with supporters, their banners hanging off the bridge and fluttering noisily in the wind. With another three-quarters of an hour to go until the start, I try to relax and watch the boats row up to the starting line at Mortlake. After what seems like ages, I can hear the crowds on the opposite side of the bridge grow excited.

'There they are!' one or two call out. I lean far forward over the green metal railing and spot Leander's first boat coming through. As winners of last year's race (or as 'Head of the River'), they are first in the overall line-up of 420-odd crews. No doubt they will have stacked their first boat with strong athletes, keen to maintain their headship. Next up is Molesey, some twenty seconds behind Leander. Several other crews follow. Then, all at once, three boats shoot out like arrows from underneath Hammersmith Bridge in the direction of Putney, the fastest of these being Cambridge. The boys look strong and light, so much lighter and easier than any of the other crews so far. They row past two crews, then another, and disappear around the bend.

By the time I get back to the boathouse, 45 boats have started, 29 have finished, over ten boats have sunk, up to a hundred oarsmen have tasted the sweet delights of the cold river Thames, the race has been cancelled, and Cambridge have come in ahead of Leander and Molesey with the fastest overall time. For us it's happy faces all round. The crew did exactly what they had planned to do. There was to be no talking about other crews until past Barnes Bridge, so as to make sure the boys kept their eyes in their own boat and focused on settling into a sustainable rhythm. As it happens, the crew ahead sank just past Barnes Bridge when hitting the rough water. From then on it was easy sailing for our boys, fighting white horses no matter what and finding themselves moving surprisingly fast, catching one boat, then the next, and before you knew it crossing the finish line with the fastest time of the lot. 'Even if the results won't stand for next year because of the cancellation, we know we found some speed. And so does Oxford. And that's all that matters.'

CHAPTER 37

Monday, 2 April; five days to go until the Boat Race

We sit down to an early morning breakfast of porridge adorned with Golden Syrup, served from an old-fashioned tin. The coffee is fresh and hot and strong. Outside it's a glorious day. We head for the KCS boathouse, where Duncan is already waiting, paper cup of latte and muffin in hand.

After the usual first outing, a paddle up to Barnes Bridge and back, Dan, Thorsten and Seb wander off to get a haircut while the rest head back to the house for lunch. When the threesome reappear, it's obvious that they've treated themselves to far more than a trim. For a princely sum they've purchased a Californian suntan off Putney High Street. Unlike the usual 'fake' tan, acquired only gradually by repeated exposure to a sunbed, theirs has been spray-painted onto their naked skins. None of us around the table had any idea that anything like it existed, but the result is stunning: they are positively orange. Such is the price of vanity.

The conversation moves from suntans to tomorrow's media event. As per tradition, both the Oxford and Cambridge crews are to appear before the media for an official weigh-in. There's no minimum or maximum weight limit for the oarsmen (bar a minimum of 55 kilograms for coxswains), but, given the often choppy Tideway waters and headwind, the heavier crew are likely to have the psychological advantage. Besides, heavy rowers tend to be taller and bigger and stronger. Can they break the all-time record for heaviest Boat Race crew? They take turns standing on a scale pinched from one of the bathrooms, while Rebecca reads out the different weights. Kip, pen and paper in hand, keeps a tally of how much the guys weigh as a crew and concludes that they might just make it – if they drink a lot.

Of course, taking on water to try to temporarily put on extra weight is nothing new. Before rowers were required to weigh in wearing nothing but their Lycras, it was easy enough to stuff pockets with tools, nuts and bolts, anything to add weight, and this confused matters for years.

That evening we sit down to watch the second part of *The Godfather*. Parts 1 and 3 will follow over the next few days, as will *Goodfellas*, *The Departed* and other twists on the world of professional crime. Dan lies stretched out on my burgundy bed with his legs on Jake's lap. Pete's in the armchair. Kip on the desk chair. Rebecca, Kieran and I sit on the soft green carpet with our backs and our heads resting against their shins and knees.

CHAPTER 38

Tuesday, 3 April; four days to go until the Boat Race

When weighing themselves again this morning, Kip, Kieran, Thorsten and Dan are disappointed to find that they're not nearly as heavy as they were last night, and head back to the table for another helping of porridge and syrup. 'We better take truck-loads of water along as well,' Dan mumbles between spoonfuls, 'got to tank up just before the weigh-in.' He pats Thorsten on the stomach. 'You're gonna be one heavy oarsman.'

'Yup, the Oxford boys are gonna be shittin' their pants,' Jake adds from the other end of the table.

Thorsten smirks. 'Okay, let's do it!' Rebecca, looking up from her broadsheet, seems bemused by the whole affair. Since when was weight-gain ever popular?

The weigh-in takes place at the Hurlingham Club, a mile or so east from KCS on the Middlesex bank of the river. Its striking Georgian clubhouse was once the cottage of a famous 18th-century physician, Dr William Cadogan, renowned for his work on gout and experiments inoculating children against chickenpox. The grounds now include 40 tennis courts, croquet and bowling lanes, a cricket pitch and golf course, indoor and outdoor swimming pools, squash courts and fitness areas, all set in 42 beautifully manicured acres. Needless to say, there's a long waiting list for would-be members of what is rather a posh affair.

The crews are shown into a large room divided into two smaller areas by a moveable makeshift wall. We can hear Oxford making their last-minute preparations from the other side of the partition. The actual weigh-in takes place in a large auditorium next door. Inside it, the stage, television cameras and lighting are set up and waiting. The Boat Race trophy – a large silver cup supported by oars – features prominently on a pedestal on the middle of the stage. Some 50-plus journalists are gathered inside. The boys meanwhile are in a world all of their own. Kieran's taken to doing press-ups. Dan and Kip take turns swelling their biceps using dumbbells. Most of the others are taking on water – 4 litres each in the cases of Dan, Jake and Thorsten. Tom is the only one not taking on significant amounts of water, something he comes to regret when they miss out on beating Oxford's 2005 record of heaviest overall crew of all time by a mere 0.15kg per oarsman. If only he'd drunk a couple of litres, they'd have entered the history books. As it is, only Thorsten breaks the record as the heaviest-ever oarsman at 110.8 kilograms, and he raises his arms in victory as ITV's Boat Race commentator, Peter Drury, announces the results.

The weigh-in over with, the guys rush first to the loo and then into civilian gear, ready to pose for pictures and to chat with the journalists already gathered in the reception area. Thorsten, needless to say, is flavour of the month, as is Rebecca, and he's photographed holding her sideways, she being less than half his own bodyweight. With her long ginger locks falling away from her face, it makes for a great Polaroid.

Rebecca herself is busy dividing her time between journalists and photographers. Having been handed control of the Blue Boat just over a week ago, she has made the broadsheets every single day. A good thing too, she thinks, as talking to journalists about the upcoming Boat Race seems to keep her mind off it. It helps her, she says, from over-analysing all the things that may, or may not, happen during the race this weekend. It's the thin silvery lining around a vast and delirious media cloud.

CHAPTER 39

Wednesday, 4 April; three days to go until the Boat Race

I boil some porridge for Rebecca, the guys, and myself on the green, heavy-set Aga. Jake walks in, his striped pyjama bottoms and T-shirt wrinkled from a restless night, thick rims resting on the ridge of his nose. Last night, as a gesture of good will, he offered to give our cooks the morning off and cook the porridge himself, but, he says apologetically, he had found it hard to get out of bed. He pours himself a mug of coffee and sits down at the breakfast table, looking inquisitively at Kip, Rebecca, Dan, Tom and Kieran perusing the papers in search of the fruits of yesterday's labour. The sports pages all headline Thorsten and Rebecca, the heaviest and lightest members of the crew, soon to sit face-to-face on the Championship course. They seem to enjoy the attention.

The main event today entails the Spare Pairs' race – pitting our two 'reserves to the reserves' against Oxford's. Each squad traditionally has not just a Blue and a reserve boat (Goldie in our case; Isis in Oxford's) but also a 'spare pair'. Should someone in the Blue Boat fall ill, he will be replaced by a Goldie oarsman, who is subsequently replaced by one of the spare pair. A fairly recent addition to the Boat Race, the Oxford and Cambridge pairs will race each other with the outgoing tide over one mile of the Championship course, from the Mile Post to the University Stone. It's a race that Oxford has won more often in recent years, and so the pressure is on for Marco Espin and Dave Hopper to prepare the ground for a clean sweep of Cambridge over Oxford.

We can just make them out as we huddle together on the balcony of KCS's boathouse. There in the distance sit Marco and Dave in a white racing shell, flanked by their Oxford counterparts. The rest of the Oxford squad are nowhere to be seen.

As soon as the umpire's flag comes down, the pairs are off. Putting into practice all they have trained for over the past months, they move on Oxford from the first stroke to gain clear water in fifteen strokes, washing them down until Oxford drift off-stream and nearly into the bank. 'I'd bloody well blown by then,' Dave tells us afterwards, 'so the race plan went right out of the window. Instead, and seeing that we already had a two-and-a-half-length advantage over Oxford, we settled into a comfortable rhythm and rowed the course.'

The squad, meanwhile, have climbed down the stairs and onto the riverbank to applaud the incoming pair. Marco smiles in response, Dave waves with one hand, the other holding on to the oar. The Oxford pair merely sit on the water, their stroke busily throwing up what remains of an early morning breakfast. What a grand start to our Boat Race campaign.

'Damn, that's good.' Tom looks on approvingly.

The evening is reserved for Cambridge's annual Press Dinner, a regular feature in Boat Race week. This year's dinner is hosted by London Rowing Club, the first of a carnival of boathouses on the Surrey side off Putney Bridge. Founded in 1856 for the specific purpose of winning medals at Henley Royal Regatta, it's currently well known as a training ground for British lightweights. We walk the 30 or so yards from KCS and make our way up the stairs into the bar, where tables are nicely laid out for a three-course dinner. Aside from two handfuls of journalists and our squad, there's an enthusiastic assembly of Old Blues – here no doubt to add that all-important bit of history and sense of place and flair to tonight's occasion.

The crew look smart in their brand-new blazers (with the exception of Kieran, who's had his for the past eight years). The Blues wear traditional woollen Cambridge blue blazers; the Goldie boys have blazers cut from a green, gold and Cambridge blue striped cloth. Out of respect for the two crews, the Old Blues sport ordinary jacket-and-tie combinations rather than the Blues blazers to which they are entitled. Someone (I don't recall who) prays silence for one of their own, David Searle. The former Cambridge Blue stands up, clears his throat, and addresses Rebecca and the boys:

'This is addressed to the two crews.

'Brad Crombie, who was President in 1999, said that training for the Boat Race was like filling a bucket of sand – one grain of sand at a time.

'Well, the bucket is full. All the work has been done.

'It's here. The Boat Race. The moment you have been preparing for these past seven months is here. The big one.

'In 67 or so hours' time you'll be on the stake boat. Shortly after that you'll be in the race that has been occupying most of your waking thoughts these past seven months.

'I don't know about you, but I feel pretty nervous just thinking about it—

'Tonight some of your guests are Old Blues and Goldies. I used to laugh when I read about the training that the crews had done 30 years before I rowed; you'd probably laugh at what we did 30 years ago in 1977.

'But in the important things there is bugger all difference between today and 1967 or 1957. These guys went through the Trials process. They did the miles and miles down at Ely and they rowed from Putney to Mortlake. They know, we know, exactly how you are feeling now and we know exactly how you will be feeling at 4.30 on Saturday.

'We are a fortunate, select bunch, and I am not being boastful here, who have rowed from Putney to Mortlake. There are something like 650 of us and 650 of them. What you can be sure of is that all of those 650 Cambridge men, and women, will have begun to get that familiar tingle a few weeks ago: 'It's Boat Race time again. It's here.' And at 4.30 on Saturday every single one of those 650 will be with you in the boat on the start and every single one of them will be rowing with you every stroke of the way.

'Now, I am tempted to say: do it for the 650.

'But there are others you are rowing for too.

'Do it for your families who have supported you through thick and thin for all these years, allowing you to follow your dream.

'Do it for your support team – all the members of the CUBC who have worked hard in their free time to get you on the start line. And then there are the people who have been with you on a daily basis: Linda, Rob, Grant, Tim, Martin, Chris, Donald and Duncan.

'But most of all – do it for yourselves. You've earned your place in your boat. You deserve to be there. This race will be a defining moment in your lives. How you will feel about the experience is entirely up to you.

'It is not our custom to wish you luck. You don't need luck. All you need is to be prepared and to have a good row.

'So go out there and have the best row of your lives ...'

David sits down to deserved and heartfelt applause. This of course is what tonight is about, or at least in part: the old showing their support for the new, reassuring them of that active, unadulterated connection between the crews of yesterday and today, and those still to come.

No sooner has David finished than I and a handful of others, as if on cue, leave the table and dash for the toilets. To my surprise, three of the older, much older, Blues have beaten me to the punch.

'The process takes damn well longer than it used to,' the oldest of them gripes while waiting for his tackle to kick into action.

'And then it does work when you don't want it to ...'

'Bloody damn frustrating if you ask me.'

CHAPTER 40

Thursday, 5 April; two days to go until the Boat Race

Today's broadsheets, keenly consumed over breakfast, continue their speculations on who might win this year's race. Cambridge are hot favourites, at least going by the bookies. Ladbrokes, Paddy Power and William Hill have Cambridge at 15/8-on to win, with Oxford at 11/8. As usual, they are offering one or two more interesting bets too. You can apparently get 25/1 with William Hill for either or both crews to sink, and 4/1 on either crew beating the course record of 16 minutes 19 seconds, set by Cambridge in 1998.

'Being underdog is so much easier,' Tom complains over toast and coffee.

For the first outing of the day I secure myself a spot on the 'Amaryllis', one of two old-fashioned mahogany boats that on race day will trail the Cambridge and Oxford crews. The bright morning sun reflects off the highly polished wood. My fellow passengers include several excitable parents (some of whom have flown in from far afield to watch their sons and daughter prepare for the big event) and the occasional Old Blue. The press have secured their own vessel, and have been at the heels of the Oxford and Cambridge crews every outing this week. Today the crews are given the opportunity to practise three proper starts from stake boats – two starts of two strokes each, followed by one fifteen-stroke start. We look on from some distance away, giving priority to the media already gathered.

While the first two starts are pretty good, the third is hugely impressive and generates appreciative grunts from the parents and Old Blues gathered in our boat. Oxford appears to be coping equally well. Their three starts were no less aggressive, nor less fast than ours, despite us rating slightly higher and Oxford looking less tidy technically. When, after fifteen strokes, Rebecca calls the 'ease the oars', Duncan and Donald move their coaching launch to within arm's length of the yellow Empacher. The crew, it seems, want a word. From where we are, it's hard to know what's going on. And so a couple of minutes pass by while the world stands still.

Then, suddenly, Duncan stands up and cups his hands around his mouth, calling out to us that the outing is over, that we are to go ashore, and that the Blue Boat will go it alone for a while. Finding Kip at the urinals some 30 minutes later, I ask him about this.

'We desperately needed some private time,' he says. 'The crew felt over-coached and suffocated and we needed space to be alone with our coxswain – to try and find our own rhythm away from the coaches and the press, and to be able to be ourselves by ourselves without worrying about who's watching or who's saying what—'

The river-front, meanwhile, is rapidly taking on a new persona as television crews sculpt their equipment around its cast-iron fences and railings, brick buildings, signposts, anything that cannot easily, or legally, be dismantled. Scaffolding upon scaffolding, supporting banners, flags, loudspeakers, electric cabling, cabins and portable lavatories. The Putney embankment is gradually transformed into a true media circus.

Back at the house, I spend some time poring over race preparations posted on the internet. Unsurprisingly, there's plenty to be had, much of it strikingly similar in orientation. This is how Oxford's chief coach Sean Bowden put it:

Once you have pushed-off to race you cannot get any stronger, fitter, tougher or learn new technical skills. Your performances will rely on your ability to row to your potential and to have the motivation necessary to push yourself physically. Your mind is not able to process large amounts of information simultaneously and therefore you have to stay focused on the essential points and only those that you can control.

External pressures and non-task-specific factors such as crowds, the opposition, parents, expectations, the outcome, etc., need to be considered beforehand and then filed away. Stay focused on the process and not the outcome. To perform in the 'big race' there will be no room for negative thoughts or self-doubt. You will be nervous, but you should be confident that you know what you are going to do and you believe in it. This is partly down to personality, but is greatly influenced by your training process.

Confidence will be based on your previous results, your training and how realistically you have set your goals. Pre-race talks need to be timed well, contain task-specific information and relate to the training process. The coach and crew will need to leave that discussion confident that there is unity of purpose and understanding. The 'blood and guts' stuff is a debatable issue and might say more about the coach than the needs of the crew. Best suffice it to say that it is preferable for the crew to be properly motivated well before they turn up to get in the boat.[29]

That afternoon the squad are told to make their way once more to London Rowing Club to meet ITV's producers and the race umpire for some important last-minute instructions. This will be ITV's third coverage of the Boat Race since having taken over the franchise from the BBC. Last night's tables and chairs stand stacked against the walls, the only noticeable residue of our media affair. Oxford are already there and waiting as we make our entrance. They look pretty much identical, decked out in plain black T-shirts with the letters 'FTT' printed in white on their backs. I look on nonplussed.

'Means "Fuck The Tabs",' whispers Kip, sitting to my right. The race, one of ITV's producers explains, will be transmitted live and so please, please, please refrain from swearing. Turning specifically to the coxswains now, he promises them a case of champagne each if they manage to control themselves. (They didn't.)

As ITV take their leave, the umpire mounts the stage. Umpiring the Boat Race, Pete Bridge explains, is the rowing equivalent of refereeing the Cup Final. The millions plugged into their televisions on 7 April will see not just the boats but, behind them, the umpire charged with a sole objective: to ensure that each crew is able to row the fastest line from their respective station (either Surrey or Middlesex). Should there be an equipment failure before Fulham Wall, either coxswain can raise an arm to stop the race. During the race, he will have to make sure that the crews stay sufficiently far apart to allow each to take the fastest line, allowing crews to get in front of each other only if there is evidence of clear water (which means at minimum half a boat length) and provided they are moving faster than the opposition. There should be no clashing of oars provided each crew stays on its station.

I look sideways at Kip, then at Rebecca, then at the boys, then at Duncan. They are looking strained, nervous. No wonder. The race is now less than 48 hours away.

CHAPTER 41

Friday, 6 April; one day to go until the Boat Race

It's half past seven in the morning and the guys and Rebecca are still asleep. Most of them went to bed early last night, with only the odd few having joined me in watching *The Departed*. Their bodies seem to have realised that they need to stock up on sleep before race day. It's almost as if there's a natural mechanism preparing the body for tomorrow's feat. Perhaps it already knows that the boys will get little sleep tonight – for they'll be nervous as hell – and so it's fuelling up on whatever it can get.

I shower, brew coffee, and sit down at the breakfast table to type up last night's handwritten notes. Dan is first to wake up.

'Mornin',' he grunts and pours himself a mug of fresh coffee.

'Porridge?'

'Sure, if you're makin' some.'

I tear open a fresh bag of oats, pour a third of it into a large pan with water and milk, and leave it to boil on the Aga. Dan, whether in anticipation of my porridge or instead of it, helps himself to cornflakes and milk and starts chomping away while browsing today's headlines. Looking through the papers is by now a familiar morning routine.

The day itself proceeds fairly uneventfully (which, after all, is the point of this week), with the customary two outings on the Tideway, all in full view of the media. Occasionally we catch a glimpse of Oxford who are boating just a few doors down, from Westminster School boathouse. When we do, we gather in front of the windows to watch them row past and shout 'Scump. Scump. Scump' (knowing full well that they can't hear us; but then we're not really shouting to be heard by them, just to hear ourselves). Like us, Oxford will have been training non-stop for seven long months and will have experienced that same rollercoaster of emotions we have. It's a great pity that one of us must face defeat tomorrow. Then again, the Boat Race wouldn't be what it is without a clear winner and a clear loser.

❖

As we sit down to a modest evening meal, I'm mindful of this being the eve of the 153rd Boat Race – that singular event to which everything to date has been but a precursor. The crew have dispatched many thousands of kilometres on the ergs and on the water, the Charles Regatta, the erg champs, Fairbairns, Fours Head, Trial Eights and Fixtures, the Head of the River Race, the Banyoles seat-races; then there's been the anxiety surrounding selection, the not knowing whether, once weighed, you're found wanting or wanted, that perpetual sense of exhaustion, of jealousy and camaraderie and competition. Will it have been worth it?

There is, I seem to recall, a scene in *True Blue* where Oxford have gathered in an oak-panelled room on the eve of the 1987 Boat Race to toast tomorrow's success. In the words of their then-coach Dan Topolski:

We got home shortly before six o'clock for the last dinner we would have together at Ranelagh Avenue. After we had eaten I asked Louise to bring in the decanter of port and each member of the crew poured himself a glass. This is an old Oxford tradition on the eve of the race, because it not only steadies the nerves, it also helps them to sleep the night before the battle. I took the telephone off the hook, shut all the doors, and began the final briefing. It was now that I would confirm our tactics and tell them how I thought the race would go.[30]

Naively perhaps, I had anticipated something similar at this present moment: something defining, epic. And yet nothing is further from the truth. Tonight's dinner is sober and wholesome, the whole affair low-key, docile and utterly anti-climactic. With Duncan, Donald and Grant having joined us, we crowd around the table, shoulder to shoulder, picking silently at our rice and fish and string beans. Not many of the boys ask for seconds. There are no final speeches, no toasts and no port. Not a word is said about tomorrow's race. It's the subject everyone seems most keen to avoid broaching, as if that makes it go away somehow. But then maybe that isn't a bad thing. It may be an anti-climactic and glum affair, but it's functional nonetheless. Trying not to make too big a deal of it may deceive them into thinking that tomorrow is just another race, no more and no less, and that tonight's sleep will be as sound as that of the night before, and the night before that.

I try to lighten the mood with a wisecrack. 'It's appropriate, isn't it, to have our last supper tonight?'

'Why?' Donald grumbles in between spoonfuls of fruit and banana yoghurt.

'Because it's Good Friday.'

'Our Lord died three hours ago—'

(Awkward.)

I tear a leaf from my Moleskine and sit down with Rebecca to write a list of everything she is to take with her to the boathouse tomorrow morning. Either last year or the year before, the Cambridge coxswain had forgotten his cox-box, forcing Martin Haycock and Quintus Travis (both Old Blues) to race back to the house on a motorbike (setting off the burglar alarm as they rifled their way through an upstairs bedroom to locate the spare cox-box) and to deliver it with only minutes to spare before the push-off. So this time around we leave nothing to chance.

Duncan and Grant slip out of the door as the crew repair to the front room to watch the third and final instalment of the *Godfather* trilogy. Ten minutes into the film, however, the guys get restless, rummage through the stack of DVDs that Tom's brought along, fish out *Goodfellas* and watch that instead. Tom himself, meanwhile, sits in the comfy armchair writing his speech for tomorrow's Blues Dinner – a traditional post-race affair that sees several generations of Blues come together for no other reason than fellowship. It's usually well attended, regardless of whether a race is won or lost. He looks up from his work occasionally, catching a glimpse of the action from the three-foot plasma screen, whether from boredom or for inspiration is unclear. Pete, Kip and Thorsten have made themselves comfortable on the cloth sofa. Dan sits on the floor, his back against Pete's shins. Linda's there too, massaging the guys in turn, either to loosen the muscles or for the sheer comfort of it. After all, there is much comfort in routine. So too in human touch, Linda's presence providing both.

We never do finish the film. One by one the boys withdraw and disappear up the stairs into their bedrooms. Occasionally I hear noises from upstairs, more so than in previous nights, people walking around the hallway and in and out of the lavatory. I expect they won't get much sleep tonight. No wonder. Looming large is the one thing they've talked and thought about for the past 199 days. I too have anticipated tonight, all the things I would and could write, except that it feels so very contrary to expectations. Tonight was no different from any other night. The mood might have been more subdued, the crew more pensive and preoccupied, any talk of tomorrow's race avoided. How un-Hollywood. And how naive I was too. Tonight's monotony is the point precisely: seven months of hard physical training boiling down to no more than an ordinary evening, indistinguishable from any other to those on the outside.

The air inside, meanwhile, is heavy with the weight of thoughts unspoken. It's the calm before the storm.

CHAPTER 42

Saturday, 7 April; BOAT RACE DAY

So this is it, I think, as I prise myself out from under the sheets and hobble up into the upstairs bathroom. As I'm towelling off, I pick up signs of life from beyond the locked door. Kip, Thorsten and Dan seem to be awake and are making their way down the stairs. I pull on some jeans and a sweatshirt and join them in the kitchen.

'Porridge anyone?' I ask unimaginatively as I walk over to the kitchen counter, grab a pan and wooden spoon, bag of oats and pint of milk.

'You nervous?' Kip asks.

'Not at all,' I lie. 'You'll look awesome today.'

'Look awesome or row awesome?' asks Thorsten.

'Both. You'll be the sexiest crew on the river today. And the fastest—'

We discuss last night's dreams over porridge. Jake dreamt about the race, he says, about the Championship course being full of obstacles – waterfalls particularly, some as high as six feet – and that they were forced to row upstream, against the tide, and even up the waterfalls, and that the boat had a little handbrake, and that during one of these climbs up the waterfall the Empacher broke, and Jake was concerned that they no longer had a boat to race in, but no one else seemed bothered, and they kept telling him things were going to be okay, but Jake was sure they weren't because they didn't have a boat any more and the race was about to begin, and … 'What the fuck did that mean?' Jake looks around the table excitedly at five chewing faces.

Thorsten hands me a piece of dry toast. I spread some butter and honey on it and take a few bites, even if I don't much feel like eating. The boys too sit around, poking listlessly into their stiffening porridge. Rebecca hasn't yet come down. She is acutely aware, as we all are, of the weight on her shoulders, and the very considerable media interest. I suspect that Oxford's coxswain Nick Brodie will have been taken by surprise too. Compared to Russ, Rebecca is a novelty, an unknown commodity, one whose racing will be difficult to predict. Better the devil you know, as they say.

Kip has wandered into the sitting room and put on the film *Seven*. Jake is in the kitchen, ironing his dress shirt for tonight's dinner. The rest are meandering about, reading a book or checking email. We will shortly head out to KCS for a brief morning outing, followed by a pasta lunch. The Tideway is like a mirror. The sun is out. It's a beautiful day. On the water, the crew look stunning: relaxed, rhythmic, serene. Rowing, done well, looks almost effortless (even if nothing could be further from the truth). As G.K. Chesterton suggested, a light supper, a good night's sleep and a fine morning have often made a hero out of the same man who, by indigestion, a restless night and a rainy morning, would have proved a coward. Let's hope this holds true today. Looking at them from the towpath, their composure belies the tempest inside, the pre-race anxiety, the terrible awareness both of being favourites to win the race and yet needing to win it to prevent Oxford from scoring a hat-trick as surprising as their mutiny twenty years ago. Oxford, as underdogs, have little or nothing to lose; after all, no one expects them to run away with the race. For Cambridge, however, the race is theirs to lose. It's a card that Tom and the boys have tried hard to downplay.

This morning there's no press boat and no coaching launch. Duncan follows at a distance, alone, as a safety boat. It's a rare chance for the crew to row as they will race, un-coached, to have no one to rely on except each other.

Back at the house, meanwhile, a hot lunch is being prepared: a simple pasta dish with tomato sauce – predictable, familiar, and anti-climatic – everything as ordinary as can be. We play-act, pretending that it's nothing but an ordinary day on the river, everyone, me included, shunning the topic that's never far from the surface. Kip watches what remains of the film. Dan sits on the sofa surfing the web. Jake walks in, back in his striped pyjamas, in time to watch Detective David Mills discover his wife's severed head in a cardboard box.

'Coffee anyone?' Susie's head has appeared from behind the doorpost. She and Dianne have been doing the cooking and cleaning over the past seven days and have proved excellent company. Her offer is greeted with enthusiasm. Brad Pitt and Morgan Freeman, meanwhile, take their leave, driving off into the distance in that empty desert landscape – empty, that is, except that it contains, in a small box, all that one of them lived for.

Kip roots around in the pile of DVDs and retrieves a complete first series of the BBC comedy series *The Office*. What better race preparation than to watch David Brent make a fool of himself at Wernham Hogg paper merchants? Out goes *Seven* and in goes *The Office*. No sooner has its familiar theme tune filled the air than the boys and Rebecca come wandering in.

As we sit around the plasma screen, we take turns commenting on the idiocy of David Brent's sidekick Gareth. Blessed with neither good looks nor tact, he's much less popular than he imagines himself to be.

BRENT TO DONNA: I'd have preferred it if you'd slept with Gareth—
DONNA: Wouldn't happen.
BRENT: Oh why, 'cos he didn't go to university?
DONNA: No, 'cos he's a little weasel-faced arse—
BRENT: Ah, you could do worse than Gareth, he hasn't missed one day, and don't call my second-in-command an arse-faced weasel.
DONNA: A weasel-faced arse.
BRENT: Same thing—

DONNA: Well no it's not. Would you rather have a face like an arse or a face like a weasel?
BRENT: A face like a weasel probably.

Thoughts of gathering crowds, television cameras, reporters, and even Oxford seem tucked away temporarily, lost in the merriment of the moment. Theirs is a stark contrast to Oxford's mental preparation last year, when they got themselves pumped up for the race with Al Pacino's moving speech in *Any Given Sunday*. Facing his team, he tells them that it all comes down to today:

> Either we heal as a team or we are going to crumble. Inch by inch, play by play, till we're finished. We're in hell right now, gentlemen, believe me. And we can stay here and get the shit kicked out of us or we can fight our way back into the light. We can climb out of hell. One inch at a time. ...
>
> We claw with our fingernails for that inch. 'Cause we know when we add up all those inches, that's going to make the fucking difference between winning and losing, between living and dying ...

It's one of those immortal celluloid speeches, ideally suited to a crew that needs to dig deep, to the underdog. It's a speech that Cambridge have used too in preparation for past races. But it isn't what they need today. Today Cambridge have one of the fastest eights on the planet. However, despite being fast on paper, it's a fragile crew too. The trick today will be to row as a unit, to trust each other fully and unreservedly, to maintain that 'Cambridge rhythm' come what may.

At 2:20pm the boys, Rebecca and I pack our kit in the van to begin our final journey to KCS, where the crowds are awaiting our arrival. After the excitement of *The Office*, calm has returned. They keep themselves to themselves as they climb into the van. After seven months of waiting, it's time to face the music. I wind down my window and turn up the radio. We snake through the now-familiar narrow Putney streets onto the Lower Richmond Road and to the Duke's Head, turning sharp left and onto the embankment. There we are stopped by a police officer.

'Do you have permission to enter the embankment?' he asks. Seb leans over excitedly as I display my pass. Vast numbers of happy supporters, crowded out from the busy embankment, have been forced onto the narrow stretch of asphalt dividing us from the boathouse, making it nearly impossible to continue driving. I put the van into first gear, look gravely at the masses in front, flick on the headlights and indicators and let the van crawl forward.

'Honk!' Seb orders. 'Keep honking and they'll move out of the way.'

'We're cool, Seb,' I say in an attempt to calm him down, and pull up as close to KCS as I can. There, among the teeming masses, is a cameraman pressing his lens into the windscreen. The big German looks at him with curiosity. The sliding door is pulled open from the outside and the boys come tumbling out, kit bags slung across their broad shoulders. Cameras flash, people call the boys by name, and good luck in the race, security personnel push against the crowd, arms spread, making way for the boys and Rebecca. I follow them up the winding concrete stairs and into the boat-house. Outside, on the upstairs balcony, parents have gathered to watch the start of the race on the stretch of river in front, and the rest of it on large television screens mounted on the inside walls for the occasion. Rebecca and the boys mostly ignore the atten-tion, moving straight through the crowds and into the changing rooms, where they swap jeans and T-shirts for black Lycra shorts and white Zephyrs with Cambridge blue collars. With blood rush-ing through my veins, and unable to stand still, I pace the area.

'Slow down,' hisses Duncan.

'Hmmm?' I turn to face him.

'You're pacing and look nervous. You don't want them to see you nervous. You don't want to make them more nervous than they already are.'

Point taken. I tell myself to slow down and take some deep

breaths. Everything from now on seems to be happening in slow motion. I pace, but pace slowly. I pick up stuff, but slowly and deliberately. I unbutton my jeans and take a pee. Slowly. Seb, by contrast, is giving his tackle a roughing over as he finishes up in the urinal next to mine, hoping no doubt to empty the tank of every last drop before the race. After all, taking a pee in full view of the world's media during warm-up is a prospect that, though not without precedent, isn't particularly attractive.

The crew sneak out of the upstairs back door to London Rowing Club. Ongoing renovations at the boathouse next door have created an obstacle course, meaning we have to climb down a set of concrete stairs to the back of KCS and into a narrow alleyway which I hadn't realised existed. From there we negotiate a paint-stained wooden ladder followed by an improvised walkway of planks laid across iron tubes, then via another ladder back into the alley and through LRC's back door. Once inside, we find ourselves in a room with a large rowing tank and several ergometers, and beyond that a much smaller room with weightlifting equipment. And it's here that we gather.

The weights room has a distinctly musty smell to it. The equipment looks old and worn from extensive use. Floor-to-ceiling mirrors line the wall to my right. Nothing but Oxford blue lines the left wall.

Rebecca and the boys are on edge. Tom looks terrified. Within the hour he'll face his demon: three Boat Race losses and the fear of losing his fourth. Seb, Thorsten and Kip too are facing the prospect of another defeat, having never yet won the race. Kieran, despite having won two previous races, is under pressure to defend his turf and to demonstrate for all that he's not yet past his sell-by date – that there's more to be had where the Olympic gold came from seven years ago.

And so we sit. And we wait.

A clock mounted on the back wall dispatches the minutes. Dan begins to stretch. So does Pete. Thorsten is working his core muscles. Rebecca merely stares, expressionless, as if deep in thought.

The public eye has weighed heavily upon her – she and Thorsten are the newest darlings of the British media. The world will be watching as she takes to the stage. Duncan talks them through the pre- and post-race logistics. He tells them what the television people will want them to do and when, and when and where we are to meet for the ride back to Putney. He talks them through preparations for tonight's dinner before reviewing the race plan once more. This is your race, he says, and it's yours to lose. Today is the culmination of much progress over seven months, and things are looking good. 'You're ready,' he concludes.

Donald agrees. These last two weeks, he says, have been particularly productive. He tells the crew they're rowing better now than ever before, and all should be well if only they stay in their rhythm. In the coin toss, Tom chose heads and lost. Oxford predictably chose the Surrey station, meaning that our crew will have to try to break them in the Fulham bend, with a strong, continued push through the Crabtree Reach, and aiming for clear water by Hammersmith Bridge. Should the plan succeed – that is, should they be in front of Oxford heading into the Surrey bend – then there's an 80 per cent chance they'll win the race, historically speaking. This is why race plans are surprisingly predictable: if on Middlesex, get in front by Hammersmith; if on Surrey, hold off Fulham bend and stay in position at Hammersmith. Though the bends of the race course cancel each other out, the Surrey bend is so long that it seems to give the Surrey station the upper hand – not least psychologically, which is probably why many, when winning the toss, have opted for Surrey.

Tom reminds them that they will have to be quick off the start. In fact, the plan all along has been to be quicker off the start than we have ever been – it's something Oxford has traditionally been better at. I'm again reminded of Topolski's advice to his 1987 crew – something that would seem as relevant for Oxford today as it was then:

The other thing going for us is that Cambridge expect to win. And however much their coach tells them to take nothing for granted, that they have a real race on their hands, deep down they know we don't have a prayer. That's why we must kill them in the first three minutes.

I don't care if you die at the Mile Post. As far as you are concerned you have just one task in life, and that is to smash Cambridge in the first mile. If they get past you after that I don't even mind, because I know you will have given your all. But please, just beat them to the Mile Post.[31]

This focus on a fast and aggressive start to the race – to try to beat Oxford at their own game – has become an increasingly prominent feature of our tactical discussions. The overall feeling seems to be that this is where Cambridge have often lost the race in recent years – and not least because of the sheer psychological wound inflicted on a crew when it realises that it has been working hard and yet is running behind. As in the practice starts this week, they will rate high and push hard, aiming to gain an advantage over Oxford as early as the Black Buoy and pushing ahead through, and shortly after, the Fulham bend.

With just ten minutes to go, and Rebecca's briefing over with, the crew take turns giving each other some last-minute counsel. The plan is clear: whatever happens, stay relaxed, trust the rhythm of the boat; don't be put off by whatever Oxford happens to be doing, but let's keep our eyes in our own boat; separate and push with the legs – nothing any more special than we've already done many times before. If we do this, we shall prevail.

'What time are we due out?' Kip asks.

'Three forty-seven.'

At precisely that hour the boys will carry the yellow Empacher out of the boathouse and onto the water, where Duncan and Grant will hold it. Then, a couple of minutes later, they will each carry their own oar out of the boathouse in full view of the television cameras. The clock chews through the hour, every new tick a reminder of the noose closing in. Kieran gets up.

'Let's do it, boys!'

On Kieran's cue we all stand up and snake our way back through the alley and across ladders and planks and scaffolding poles into the downstairs back of the KCS boathouse. From here on, the scene's choreographed by a young woman in a red fleece, walkie-talkie in hand, and very much in charge. The programme's been delayed by a couple of minutes, she tells us. The boat's already on the water. Things will be 'live' from now on, she reminds us – as if anyone needed reminding. The boys find their oars, each marked with their names in thick black ink, and line up in two rows: Thorsten and Seb first; Kip and Dan last. Rebecca last of all. The tension hangs like thick smoke in the air. Someone farts. Everyone stands nervously, oar in hand, facing the noisy crowds outside, and beyond them the brown tidal river. Tom looks particularly nervous. Of course he's got more at stake than anyone else – the journalists, no doubt, will make much of the weight on his shoulders of three previous Boat Race defeats.

'Ready? Then out you go,' commands the lady in red.

Like eight dapper soldiers, the crew march out of the boathouse and into the limelight, hearts in their mouths, palms sticky with perspiration. Four-point-four million people will be watching this live in the United Kingdom alone, and many more across the world. Rebecca is last out, looking straight ahead as if oblivious to all the attention that has been poured over her by the media these past two weeks, and even now. Her eyes, puffy for lack of sleep, tell of the terrible strain she's under. Together the crew march down the sloping embankment towards the Empacher, laid out calmly on this unusually placid stretch of the river. I follow on behind, leaving enough time so as not to interfere with the cameras. The boys get in the boat, chuck their rubber boots onto the concrete, and fasten the Velcro on their shoes, their oar handles tucked underneath their armpits all the while to keep the boat stable. I collect their boots and carry them over to the Tin Fish, where Grant and Linda sit already waiting. We'll ferry them along to Mortlake so they'll be waiting for them on arrival at the finish line.

I pick up fragments from Peter Drury's television commentary over the loudspeakers that line the length of the embankment. '... Tom James ... his fourth and final boat race ... having lost three ... heavy on his shoulders ...' Tom, however, remains entirely unfazed, focused intently on fastening his shoes.

On Rebecca's command they push off in the direction of Wandsworth Bridge for a planned 40-minute warm-up. The crowds go wild as they do so.

'Come on Cambridge!'

'That's it, Cambridge!'

'Good luck, boys!'

'Go get them, lads!'

'Go, Cambridge!'

Rebecca and the boys seem unmindful of the world erupting around them.

I join Grant and Linda in the Tin Fish. We'll be driving along-side several other launches following the Goldie–Isis race. Their wellies too are with us in the launch. This is pure adrenaline, pure excitement, I think, and take a few snaps of the crowds, several rows thick, lining the embankment. It doesn't get better than this. The weather is stunning. I loosen the collar of my jacket to let in the refreshing April breeze and pull my white cap a little tighter around my head so that it won't be blown off by the wind as we pick up speed.

Grant points at the stake-boats with one hand, the other hold-ing tight to the throttle of the outboard engine. As Goldie and Isis come past us, he revs up the engine and we're off too, keeping to about 50 yards from the racing crews. Things are boding well for Goldie: they're on the Surrey station (having won their toss) and are first into the Fulham bend. On the Crabtree Reach they're able to get a length on Isis and find clear water, getting a full length ahead by Hammersmith and into the Surrey bend first, increasing their advantage first by two, then three, then four, and ultimately five lengths before passing the University Post at Mortlake.

What a fantastic race to watch! We all knew that Goldie were fast but expected the opposition to be fierce. Yet the crew did away with them without too much difficulty. Bakes, responsible for coaching Goldie, joins in the cheering with enthusiasm. And justly so. He has much to be proud of. These are his boys, after all. The noise from the crowds at Mortlake, and from the launches following the crews, is deafening.

But Goldie's magnificent victory over Isis will vanish into thin air unless the Blue Boat is victorious too. For however many races they may have won this year, none matters as much as winning the Boat Race. And history will record none but today's result. If all goes well, Cambridge will have turned the tables on Oxford, having redeemed last year's embarrassing defeat.

I'm as nervous as hell.

Grant drives the Tin Fish up the shallow gravel slope of Mortlake's boathouse, where we clamber out and walk the 30 or so yards towards a canvas pavilion. It's noisy inside. Several hundred supporters, tall glasses of champagne clutched in their hands, are gazing at large flat-screen television panels, six in all, where the Boat Race will shortly feature. Despite my 6ft 3in, I have to balance on my toes to catch a glimpse of the plasma screen, eight feet away and the crowd about that many rows deep. No sooner have I secured a precious two square feet than the race is on. It's actually happening.

The crowd, merry to begin with, is growing concerned. Things are not what the Cambridge supporters had hoped for. Oxford have produced the quicker start and, despite the first bend being in our favour, are already three seats up. On my right a Dark Blue jumps up and down excitedly as Oxford approach the Surrey bend. As Oxford's coxswain Nick Brodie knows full well, if they can maintain their early advantage over Cambridge, he should be able to control the racing line through that long and formidable bend.

Entering the second bend while on the outside racing line and lagging behind, Rebecca is at a distinct disadvantage. Oxford is likely to opt for a wide entry into the bend to try to push us even wider and out of the stream before tucking sharply back into the Surrey bank. And so hers is the unenviable task not just of sticking firmly to her own racing line but of 'holding' Oxford as they try to break away and move on ahead. If Cambridge succeed in keeping up with their rivals, they might just break Oxford's spirits. After all, this is Oxford's big opportunity to win the race.

Even as these worries must be preoccupying her, Rebecca stays admirably calm. And in a way she has to: any nervousness on her part will be picked up by the crew and risks disturbing their rhythm. It's in moments like these that psychology comes into play. She's here today precisely because everyone felt she would be the best person to handle just this sort of situation.

Predictably, Nick Brodie nudges Oxford over. The crews draw perilously close, their oars nearly clashing. Rebecca stays calm and holds her line. Oxford is warned to move over and, as Brodie obediently puts the rudder on, Cambridge press and gain a couple of feet. But these twenty or so inches on Oxford are worth miles in psychological terms. With renewed confidence they gradually, stroke by stroke, pull level with Oxford. Peter Drury, Tim Foster, Wayne Pommen and James Cracknell provide the running commentary:

'... Rebecca is still quite relaxed there but things are going to get very urgent for the Cambridge crew very soon if they let Oxford slip away any more – there are some here that would say that an Oxford win would be the biggest upset since the year of the mutiny, 1987. Oxford have a lead – now think back a year and how the scene changed from here. Cambridge hit a wall of water, where Mother Nature took up her oar and pelted them with wind and waves, where the issue of Oxford's pump and Cambridge's lack of one became an issue, where the result was put beyond doubt – it is still very much in doubt now – there are no adverse conditions – what we've had is a clean race so far – I've been very impressed with the Oxford crew – they may not have the individuals, but they have the team, and they're rowing very well together. Cambridge is a little longer in style and some would say they're more efficient, and they have been hanging on in the bend – a moment ago I wouldn't have been able to tell you which crew I'd rather be in, but at this point things are starting to look good for Cambridge – they've almost pulled back level – two more minutes and they will have the inside advantage of the next bend – the point being, ladies and gentlemen, that Cambridge had to hang on around the big Surrey bend – provided they're more or less level, the final portion of the race will favour Cambridge ...'

And, providentially, it was precisely *here* that Duncan saw that dolphin a month ago. It was here too that Cambridge knew their recently-found rhythm would prevail over Oxford's aggression. Even as their start was disappointing, the crew knew that they couldn't afford to be distracted, that even as they were strong on paper they were fragile as a crew – that victory could be theirs, but only so long as they remained confident in each other and steadfast in the belief that this rhythm would raise their game above that of the sum of the individuals.

Now, some three miles into the race, and with Barnes Bridge in sight, Cambridge begin to put clear water between the crews for the first time in the race. Knowing that Oxford haven't done enough to break their spirits, and Oxford now realising that their Surrey advantage is running out, Cambridge take the lead and in 30 powerful strokes gain a boat length on their rivals.

A few minutes later they cross the finish line – a boat length and a quarter ahead. What an epic race! What a brilliant affair.

As Rebecca and the guys cross the finish line, Pete's arms go up in victory. Thorsten falls back into Seb's lab, exhausted and pale, the blood drained from his face, too tired even to muster a smile. Seb hangs forward, casting a shadow over his friend and stroke, small rivers of sweat trickling from his face onto Thorsten's. Kieran hangs forward too, mouth open, exhausted. Tom, behind him, has fallen into Jake's lap, arms stretched and around Jake's neck. Jake leans forward. There's no smile here either, just exhaustion. Pete's the only one capable of celebrating their hard-fought win over Oxford this sunny April afternoon. And of course there's Rebecca too, delirious with her well-deserved victory. She splashes water over her boys but they're too worn out to feign a response. Then, gradually, one by one, they look up and raise their arms. But Tom just sits there, looking at us gathered in thick, sticky rows at Mortlake. What vindication. What better year than in his year as President. What a moment this must be for him – 'fourth time lucky, after suffering three previous defeats at the hands of the old Dark Blue enemy,' as Dan Topolski will report in tomorrow's *Observer*. And yet, curiously, Tom neither waves nor shouts nor punches the air like the others. He merely sits and stares, as if absorbing the moment, committing it to memory in all its colour and vibrancy. He is the man of the moment. His inner demon's slain. A new dawn has broken. It's morning: the beginning of a new chapter to the same old book, every new page better than the pages before it.

I watch the crew paddle up to the gravel slope, Rebecca giving her final orders before climbing out. No sooner are they out than they're pounced on by supporters and media alike. This is the moment they've been working so hard for, and it's finally here. It really is here. What a day. What a glorious day. So much drunken merriment. I embrace them and they me.

Oxford, meanwhile, are approaching the gravel too. Their anguish is painfully evident. They fought hard. They too anticipated this day, having dispatched as many kilometres on the ergs as we have, having lifted as many weights for as many repetitions, having made as many sacrifices. And they were far tougher than we ever imagined them to be, showing great strength and resolve – making us believe for a moment that they had it in them to beat our crew. I cannot help but feel sorry for them. The Boat Race is, in many ways, all about taking part – to be counted a Blue – and yet for the loser it's truly a terrible ordeal. I pick out one or two encouragements from the crowd as their crew get out of the boat. One journalist takes their President, Ejsmond-Frey, aside for a brief post-mortem.

Rebecca and her boys are ushered onto the stage for the award ceremony. They're each handed a bottle of champagne, the contents of which is used to hose each other down, and Tom in partic-ular, now barely able to see through the torrents of bubbly, yet laughing uncontrollably all the while. He lifts the silver trophy as the crowds cheer and cameras flash. I look on from behind a cheap plastic fence.

When the award ceremony is finally over, and Rebecca dunked in the river, the media frenzy begins all over again. One by one the boys peel off into the crowd, accompanied by one or more journal-ists, old-fashioned tape recorders drawn, ready to pounce. They seem to enjoy the attention. Kieran empties a bottle of champagne on the already wet and shivering Rebecca. Jake poses for snaps with his parents. I grab hold of a half-empty bottle of champagne and join in.

The van ride back to Putney is awesome. It's beers all round. Seb winds down his window and, arms clinging to the roof of the Transit, heaves his body out of the van, shouting 'Cam-bridge! Cam-bridge!' to all who want to hear. An elderly woman, crossing the street in front of us, takes issue with Seb's enthusiasm, wonder-ing out loud whether all this noise is really necessary. But she doesn't understand, does she? She doesn't know how important this is for the five returning Blues, and for Jake, and for Pete and Dan, and for Rebecca, and for Duncan. And yet what does it matter anyway? Does the joy of the moment not override social norms? Is this not the least the crew deserve right now? Duncan, all the while, keeps pumping the horn to much approval. Thorsten too opens his window, waving his Cambridge blue toggle top to passers-by. It matters not that 'one of these days the last wisps of glory that trail behind him will vanish into thin air and he will simply be one of us'.[32] The pedestrians (many of whom have pre-sumably just watched the race) respond positively, cheering us on as we snake past, intoxicated by today's victory. I catch Duncan smiling in the rear-view mirror.

'Mortlake to Putney is so much more fun than the other way around!' Jake shouts above the noise. Like this it is. This feels bloody good.

We stop the van just before reaching the Putney embankment, allowing Rebecca and the crew a victory parade towards friends and family at KCS. The crowds still gathered at the boathouses are elated, waving their arms as they see the crew approach. We head for the showers. I lend Kip my towel and socks, deodorant, after-shave and hair gel. Towels and blazers hang draped over rusty metal lockers. Tom tiptoes through the inch-deep muddy water covering the floor. This is the most wonderful day of his life, he shouts across the room. Little Lycra islands appear and disappear among the dripping crowd and serve as useful stepping stones. Duncan stands fiddling with his bow tie. Goldie's Tobias, wearing nothing but boxers, lends him a helping hand.

I stand around naked, as they are, unashamed of my nakedness.

EPILOGUE

Despite all the knowledge and academia within Cambridge University, the Boat Club has never taken much advantage of its surroundings in terms of research and development. Mark's request to follow our training and hopefully give us some feedback in terms of our team dynamics was therefore met with a very positive response.

Rowing has always been a sport for creativity and invention in order to squeeze every last inch out of each stroke. The number of ludicrous schemes that coaches have concocted to the astonishment and despair of their athletes are recounted all too often in post-dinner speeches or between rowers sharing experiences. So even with this in mind, Duncan and I invited Mark to join the Cambridge squad for the 2007 campaign to beat Oxford – a decision which both of us can resoundingly say we were glad to have made.

The first time Mark came to the boathouse, one could have been forgiven for assuming that the actual ethnographer had sent his junior assistant in his place. Looking a good fifteen years younger than his age suggested, with his characteristic rainbow-coloured rucksack and bohemian soul patch goatee, Mark was not your typical Cambridge Fellow. He consequently fitted into the squad with ease and became a great friend and advisor to many of the athletes.

This year more than any, perhaps, warranted the need for a counsellor of sorts on board. The combination of five returning losing Blues of international stature, a new coach having lost his first race, and a President who had raced in three Boat Races and had yet to win his first, would inevitably generate its fair share of complexes and issues. There aren't any secrets to winning a race – row better and row harder. Watching a race, it's easy to see the difference in one boat being superior to another, but it's a long and arduous route of debate and compromise that gets you there.

Throughout my time on the Cambridge squad, one of the more significant challenges for any coaching staff, specifically to the Boat Race, has been uniting the very different personalities, ages and levels of experience that each athlete brings to the start of the year. The season itself is very short, and by the time the race has been and gone, only then do you feel that you have truly come to know the people you're rowing with.

For myself, the joy and relief of Cambridge winning that day cannot be described. Mark was a huge asset to the Club during my final year and helped me personally to get through some of the tougher times in the season. However, the most rewarding aspect of Mark's presence was seeing him inadvertently transform from an impartial observer into as much of a member of the squad as any one of us. It has also been a great privilege to have my final and only winning year documented in such detail, the essence of CUBC and the characters of everyone involved captured so accurately. On behalf of the team I would like to thank him for devoting such time and effort to helping us win this year.

Tom James, President of the Cambridge University Boat Club,
2006–07

NOTES

1   David Lodge in *Small World* (Penguin, 1985).
2   I remember a wonderful line from a fellow ethnographer (I believe it was John Van Maanen) suggesting that ethnography is culture in black and white.
3   Paraphrasing S.T. Coleridge, in *Coleridge's Notebooks: A Selection* (Oxford University Press, 2002).
4   Sebastian Faulks in *Human Traces* (Vintage, 2006), pp. 38–9.
5   The concept of flow was popularised by University of Chicago psychologist Mihaly Csikszentmihaly in his classic *Flow: The Classic Work on How to Achieve Happiness* (Rider & Co., 2002).
6   G.C. Drinkwater MC (OUBC) and T.R.B. Saunders (CUBC), *The University Boat Race*, Official Centenary History (Cassell, 1929), p. 7.
7   G.C. Drinkwater in *The Boat Race* (Blackie, 1939).
8   Matthew Pinsent, quoted in Julian Andrews, *What it Takes … to Earn Your Place: Celebrating Rowing Through the 150th Oxford v. Cambridge Boat Race* (Third Millennium Publishing, 2004).
9   Hugh Matheson's beautiful essay appears in *Battle of the Blues*, ed. Christopher Dodd and John Marks (P to M Limited, 2004), including the reference to Boris Rankov's pondering on the Macedonian spear.
10 As G.C. Drinkwater (1939) points out, there are in fact three officially recorded times for this race, the 14m 30s being the longest one. The race was restarted, which may have resulted in differences in time-keeping. The letter from Wordsworth to Merivale is reproduced in full in G.C. Drinkwater (1939), pp. 13–14.
11 Donald Legget, quoted in *Battle of the Blues* (2004).
12 The reference to Brezhnev's generals stems from one of my favourite contemporary novelists, J.M. Coetzee, and his *Diary of a Bad Year* (Harvill Secker, 2007). His own reference to Brezhnev's generals as sitting 'somewhere in the urinals' is ambiguous, yet has stuck with me and, for equally ambiguous reasons, perfectly captured my mood that morning.
13 Robin Williams, quoted in *What it Takes … to Earn Your Place* (2004).
14 From Kafka's 'A Fasting-Artist', as quoted in Martin Amis, *Experience* (Vintage, 2001), p. 79.
15 From Philip Larkin's 'This Be The Verse', in *Collected Poems* (Faber & Faber, 2003). Slightly paraphrased.
16 W.G. East, 1904.
17 From http://www.theboatrace.org/article/newsandmedia/latestnews/newscambridge t8report06
18 Jack Kerouac in *Big Sur* (Panther Books, 1980).
19 Pete had won rowing trophies with London University and ended up in fourth place for Great Britain at the 2006 World University Championships in Lithuania.
20 Philip Larkin, untitled poem, in *Collected Poems*, edited by Anthony Thwaite (Faber & Faber, 2003), p. 35.

21 Søren Kierkegaard, 'Repetition', in *Kierkegaard's Writings*, Vol. 6 (Princeton University Press, 1983).

22 Poem by the religious writer Charles Swindoll.

23 Saul Bellow in *Seize the Day* (Penguin Modern Classics, 1984), pp. 117–18.

24 From Saul Bellow's *Humboldt's Gift* (Penguin Classics, 2007), p. 312.

25 Jack Kerouac in *Big Sur* (Panther Books, 1980), p. 26.

26 Paraphrasing John Simpson in 'Tiananmen Square', in *The Granta Book of Reportage* (Granta, 2007), p. 243.

27 'Competent Jerks, Lovable Fools, and the Formation of Social Networks', *Harvard Business Review*, Vol. 83, No. 6, June 2005.

28 From *The Game* by Neil Strauss (Canongate Books, 2006), p. 78.

29 As originally published in *Regatta* magazine. Available online at: http://www.rowingservice.com/regatta/99-bowden.html

30 Dan Topolski and Patrick Robinson, *True Blue: The Oxford Boat Race Mutiny* (Bantam Books, 1990).

31 Dan Topolski, *True Blue* (1990).

32 From J. M. Coetzee's *Slow Man* (Vintage, 2006), p. 182.

Index